Builders of Annapolis

By the Same Author

Wisconsin: The Story of the Badger State
Thomas Jefferson
Jefferson's America, 1760–1815
America: A History of the United States
Representative Americans: The Colonists
Representative Americans: The Revolutionary Generation
Chesapeake Politics, 1780–1800
The Old Republicans: Southern Conservatism in the Age of Jefferson

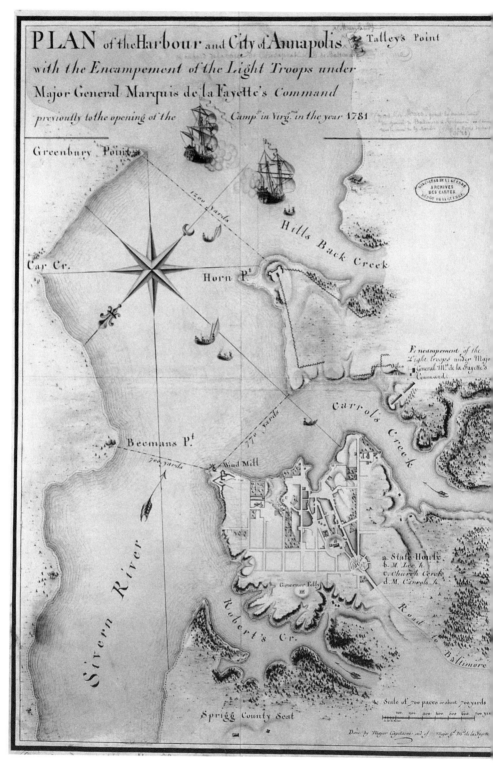

PLAN of the Harbour and City of Annapolis.

with the Encampement of the Light Troops under

Major General Marquis de la Fayette's Command

previously to the opening of the Camp. in Virg. in the year 1781

Talley's Point

Greenbury Point

Car Cr.

Hills Back Creek

Horn P.t

Encampement of the Light Troops under Majo.r General M.ris de la Fayette's Command.

Beemans P.t

1200 Yards

770 Yards

700 yards

Wind Mill

Carrols Creek

a. State House.
b. M. Lee h.
c. Church Cereh.
d. M. Carrols h.

Sivern River

Governor Folly

Robert's Cr.

Road to Baltimore

Scale of 700 paces or about 700 yards

Sprigg County Seat

Done by Major Capitaine and of Major Ge.l M.ris de la Fayette

Builders of Annapolis

Enterprise and Politics in a
Colonial Capital

Norman K. Risjord

MARYLAND HISTORICAL SOCIETY

BALTIMORE

MARYLAND HISTORICAL SOCIETY
201 West Monument Street
Baltimore, Maryland 21201
Founded 1844

First Edition

Manufactured in the United States of America

ISBN 0-938420-60-7

LIBRARY OF CONGRESS CATALOGING-IN-PUBLICATION DATA

Risjord, Norman K.
    Builders of Annapolis : enterprise and politics in a colonial capital /
Norman K. Risjord. — 1st ed.
    p.   cm.
    Includes bibliographical references and index.
    ISBN 0-938420-60-7 (alk. paper)
    1. Annapolis (Md.)—Biography.   2. Maryland—History—Colonial
period, ca. 1600-1775—Biography.   3. Elite (Social Sciences)—
Maryland—Annapolis—Biography.   4. Artisans—Maryland—Annapolis—
Biography.   I. Maryland Historical Society.   II. Title.
    F189.A653A29   1997
920.0752'56—cd21   97-44607
                                                                              CIP

∞ The paper used in this publication meets the minimum requirements
of the American National Standard for Information Sciences —
Permanence of Paper for Printed Library Materials, ANSI Z39.48-1984.

COVER:
Annapolis in 1784. Watercolor by Charles Melbourne.
Maryland State Archives

COVER AND FRONTISPIECE:
"Plan of the Harbor and City of Annapolis..."
Commissioned by Marquis de Lafayette in 1781.
Maryland State Archives

INSIDE COVERS:
View of Annapolis by E. Sachse and Co., 1858.
Maryland State Archives

To my granddaughter Hannah,
a builder of the next century

Contents

List of Illustrations

Preface

This book follows a pattern I started with my *Representative Americans* books. Each chapter is a biographical sketch of an individual — or of linked individuals — who contributed to the development of Annapolis in the eighteenth century. By choosing persons from different walks of life — politicians, lawyers, a physician, a printer, a cabinetmaker — I aim also to provide a portrait of life in Annapolis at that time. The title *Builders of Annapolis* has a double meaning. It refers to the people who made Annapolis a major political, social, and cultural center in the years before the American Revolution, but it also refers significantly to the structures they built. The chapter on William and Mary Paca is, in some ways, as much the story of their house as of them. The whole is preceded by a Prologue which seeks to portray life and living conditions in Maryland at the time that Annapolis was founded.

Every author owes many debts. Members of the history department at the United States Naval Academy read the opening chapter on Governor Francis Nicholson and saved me from a number of errors in European history. Mary Cory, curator of the Paca House, supplied me with the reports of the historical architects who have examined the house for the Historic Annapolis Foundation, and she gave me a very helpful reading of the Paca chapter. Alecia Parker, director of research for the Historic Annapolis Foundation, gave me access to numerous documents and pictures. I am also obliged to the helpful staff of the Nimitz Library of the Naval Academy, and to its director Richard Werking, who was a teaching assistant of mine at the University of Wisconsin a quarter of a century ago.

As always, my deepest thanks go to my wife Connie, who read the typescript with her usual thoughtful care and provided me with a thousand helpful suggestions.

N. K. R.

Annapolis
May 1997

Prologue

❦

Maryland in 1700

Although nearly seventy years old at the turn of the eighteenth century, the Maryland colony still appeared very much a wilderness plantation.* Its population of 30,000 was fairly evenly distributed along the shores and estuaries of Chesapeake Bay. By 1700, two counties on the Eastern Shore, Somerset and Talbot, were the most heavily populated in the province with populations, respectively, of 5,400 and 4,860. Anne Arundel on the Western Shore (with 4,100 people) was third, and St Mary's (3,500), the original point of settlement, was fourth. With an abundance of optimism, the proprietor had established counties (Baltimore and Cecil) at the head of the bay in the mid-seventeenth century. Each had about 2,000 people in 1700. Prince George's County, founded in 1696, was on the frontier; its slender population of 2,300 clung to the banks of the Patuxent and Potomac Rivers. The land west of the Monocacy River was considered Indian country.

Even in the well-populated parts of the colony the landscape had a wild and untamed appearance. One newcomer sailing up the bay said the shoreline looked "like a forest standing in water." Because land was cheap, it was more profitable to rotate fields than to rotate crops. Tobacco was the staple of the colony's trade and almost the only source of income. Its culture was very labor intensive. Seedlings, sprouted in a shady forest loam, had to be transplanted in early summer to the open field and cultivated frequently with a hoe. Worms, which appeared in mid-summer, had to be picked off one by one. Harvesting was a matter of plucking and carefully drying each tobac-

---

*Although we think today of "plantation" as a large Southern farm, its original meaning was a settlement in a new country or region.

xiii

co leaf. A man, whether slave or free, could handle only about three acres of tobacco in a year. The soil was exhausted after about three years; the plot was abandoned and a new one cleared. The abandoned land was allowed to go to weeds and brush for twenty years, while the planter's cattle and hogs, who roamed freely in the woods, slowly restored its fertility. To maintain continuous production, a planter thus had to possess fifty or sixty acres for each worker he placed on the land. The result was an untidy landscape that seemed to travelers devoid of population.

Larger planters with access to the water sold their tobacco to the master of a passing vessel or sometimes consigned it directly to a merchant in London. Farmers in the interior had to roll the hogsheads to the docks. Each hogshead became self-transporting with a pin inserted at each end and a hoop shaft connecting the pins to the collars of horses. The horses then pulled the tobacco to the nearest wharf along a "rolling road," which was the colony's basic highway system. Main roads that led to a county courthouse or a place of worship were required by law to be cleared and grubbed of brush to a width of twenty feet. Such "highways" were marked by two notches on trees on either side of the road.

Tobacco harvested and stored for shipment represented credit that could be used for money. The larger planters traded their tobacco in England for bills of exchange or manufactured goods. The bills of exchange circulated in America as money valued in British sterling. Smaller planters sold their hogsheads to brokers at the landings. The brokers paid them in tobacco notes. Each note specified the net weight received, the name of the warehouse, and the type of tobacco. The notes passed from hand to hand as legal tender. Colonists valued their goods, paid their taxes, and settled their debts with tobacco notes.

The direct exchange with the mother country from the planters' wharves retarded the growth of towns and cities. The only hamlet of consequence in 1700, newly founded Annapolis, had fewer than one hundred inhabitants. St Mary's City, the previous capital, which had never consisted of more than a few taverns and ordinaries, simply vanished after losing the government. Some well-to-do planters kept stores stocked sparingly with imported goods, but otherwise local trade was a matter of neighborhood barter, as people learned through word of mouth who had a cow, a hog, or corn to spare.

The annual income from tobacco sales of a common planter ranged from £10 to £15. The largest planters in that rude frontier society realized an annual income of £200 to £250 from their tobacco. The wealthier planters also had other ways of making money. Some practiced law or kept stores, selling stocks of imported goods to their neighbors. Those with extra cash functioned as bankers, taking mortgages on their neighbors' properties. Money was ever scarce in the colonies, and money-lending was highly profitable. Interest was fixed by law at 6 per cent for money loaned in tobacco and 8 per cent for money loaned in pounds sterling. These non-farm activites generated an additional £200 to £300 a year for the wealthy. Government service was also quite lucrative, for public officials — surveyors in the land office, for instance — were allowed to charge fees for their services. Placemen in the higher echelons of the government could increase their annual incomes by as much as £500. Most of the great fortunes of eighteenth-century Maryland were founded on government service.

Maryland's was a population predominantly of men, most of whom had come to the colony as servants. The cost of a voyage from England to the Chesapeake was £6 sterling. This price was beyond the means of most ordinary Englishmen. As a result, many men and women who wanted to move to America for a new start in life indentured themselves for a period of service of four or five years to pay for their passage across the Atlantic. Criminals who were transported to the Chesapeake as a punishment (and to relieve crowded English jails) had seven-year terms of service.

Most servants were destined for work in the tobacco fields, and the planters naturally preferred men to women. Of the 30,000 people counted in a census of 1704, only about 7,000 were women. The women who came as servants had to work off their time before they could marry, unless their time was purchased by a planter eager for a mate. The scarcity of women and late marriages combined to cause a relatively low birthrate. Indeed, the birthrate lagged behind the death rate until after 1700. Population expanded only because of new arrivals from England. Two out of three adult men in 1700 were immigrants from the British isles.

Because of the shortage of females about 20 per cent of Maryland men died without ever marrying. The shortage, on the other hand, worked to the advantage of women. If a female servant's indenture was not purchased by a prospective husband, she was virtually certain to find one when she had served out her time. There were men aplenty and no father or brothers about to monitor her behavior or limit her choice. Court records indicate that about a fourth of immigrant women whose marriages were recorded were pregnant at the time.

The daughters born of these immigrant marriages wrought a radical change in the colony's demographic profile. Native-born women married much earlier than immigrants, usually by the time they were eighteen. With more years of fertility they gave birth to more children, and, although infant mortality remained high, the population gradually began a natural increase after 1700.

The wills drafted by husbands are a further indication that women in America were highly regarded. The law required that a widow be left with a third of her husband's land and personal possessions, but only about a fourth of the men left their widows with merely the minimum required. If there were no children, a man almost always left his entire estate to his widow, and, significantly, he rarely felt the need of a male executor to supervise her management of it. Most men made no specific provision for their children, other than that they be given some education, trusting their widows to see that the children received fair portions. The wealthier fathers often conveyed a portion of their estates to their sons and daughters when they married.

The wife's dower rights in her husband's estate reflected her economic importance to the family. If a farmer was too poor to afford a servant (about a fifth of all farmers were in this class), his wife had to help out in the tobacco fields. Even if a wife had only household duties, her contribution was significant. She maintained a vegetable garden, milked the cow, slaughtered the pigs, and made butter and cheese. Food preparation was hard and time-consuming. Corn, a staple of the diet, had to be ground by hand with mortar and pestle because there were few water-powered mills in the colony. She sewed clothing and did the laundry in a tub with homemade soap. One is led to wonder how the many men who never found wives managed to survive at all.

The black slave population of Maryland in 1700 mirrored the white population in two respects — it was made up mostly of recent immigrants and was predominantly male. The first black servants in the Chesapeake were brought in from the West Indies. They were few in number and worked side by side with white servants in the tobacco fields. In the last two decades of the seventeenth century African slavery replaced white servitude as the colony's basic labor force, and most of the blacks were imported directly from Africa.

Black immigrants suffered the same "seasoning" process as whites. About one in four died during the first year in the Chesapeake. Because Africans possessed some native immunity to malaria, they suffered less from that scourge than the white population. They were unaccustomed, however, to the cold winters, and many succumbed to respiratory illnesses. New arrivals were far more likely to run away than blacks born in the Chesapeake or the West Indies. Since slavery existed in all the colonies, the only true avenue to freedom was the wilderness. By the early eighteenth century the Maryland Assembly was complaining of blacks who escaped to live with the Indians, and it ordered that any slave who ran beyond the Monocacy River was to be branded on the forehead and have an ear lopped off.

The birthrate among blacks also paralleled that of whites. As with the white population, black males substantially outnumbered black females. Because most females came to the Chesapeake in their mid-twenties, they gave birth, on average, to only three children, with only two surviving to adulthood. Accordingly, the birthrate did not begin to exceed the death rate until some time after 1720. The development of an Afro-American community took even longer. Most Maryland plantations were modest affairs; half of them had fewer than twelve slaves. In such quarters a family unit consisting of a husband, wife and children was uncommon, and the slaves did not control enough space of their own to develop a society apart from the master. Not until the middle of the eighteenth century, when the natural increase in population permitted the development of families and kinship networks and plantations of several hundred slaves made their appearance, can we speak of an Afro-American culture in Maryland.

Although most families lived in primitive isolation, neighborhood locales maintained a sense of community. Because the community was small in number, each family was intimately aware of the lives and fortunes of its neighbors. They rendered mutual aid, bore witness to land transactions, and cared for children in times of sickness. This set of relationships was typical of neighborhood communities elsewhere in America and in England. But in one respect the Maryland communities were unique — they lacked churches. Lord Baltimore had decreed religious toleration shortly after the first colonists arrived. Without state support, religion languished. Although most of the first settlers were Roman Catholics, Protestants soon outnumbered Catholics in the colony, but the Church of England made no effort to minister to their needs. Between 1634 and 1690 only six Anglican ministers are known to have arrived in the colony. During the Puritan Revolution in England in the 1640s and 1650s, a substantial number of Puritans settled in Maryland. Their churches followed the Presbyterian model, but they made little effort to add to their numbers by converting fellow colonists. The vast majority of Marylanders were simply unchurched in 1690.

The Glorious Revolution of 1688–89 ended the Restoration reign of James II, deprived the Baltimore proprietors of their charter, and rendered Maryland a royal colony under William of Orange. The Church of England became by law the official church of the colony. That change brought to Maryland the centerpiece of the English neighborhood community, the parish vestry. The vestry, consisting of fifteen to twenty of the most prominent men in the community, were elected to the post by their neighbors. The vestry governed the church, chose the pastor, and arranged for his pay in tobacco. The vestry never became as important in Maryland as it did in neighboring Virginia, but the arrival of Anglican churches in the eighteenth century did help focus Maryland communities. On Sundays all gathered at the nearest church, whether or not they attended the services. Visiting after church became an established custom. It was a time for exchanging news, discussing politics, and organizing games, all accompanied by smoking and the consumption of cider and beer.

Social behavior was regulated more by neighborhood consensus than by legal authority. The repeated violation of community norms brought heavy penalties in a society where neighbors were heavily dependent upon one another for mutual aid. County courts were made up of justices of the peace, who were themselves planters of the neighborhood. They and their juries were apt to deal harshly with repeated offenders. Even the most law-abiding citizen depended heavily on his reputation in the community when he sought credit from a merchant, stepped forward to administer an estate, or stood for public office.

The provincial government was notoriously weak and unstable before 1700. High mortality and a low birthrate meant that the governing institutions — the Council, the Assembly, and the Provincial Court — was staffed by immigrants. Tenure in office was brief; experience was a rare commodity. There was no collective memory or body of precedent for decision-making. All this changed after 1700 with an increase in the native-born population. The Assembly elected in 1704 was the first in the colony's history in which a majority of the members were either native-born or had arrived in Maryland as children. The amount of property they possessed averaged eight hundred acres and ten slaves. Older, wealthier, and better educated than their predecessors, such legislators also brought to office the benefits of experience as county justices of the peace or church vestrymen. They were, in short, the kernel of a social and political élite that emerged in Maryland in the course of the next twenty-five years.

This élite centered in Annapolis, the provincial capital where, by the mid-eighteenth century, a remarkable collection of merchants, lawyers, and tradesmen would form one of the most sparkling communities in British America. The stories of these people, neighbors of one another, appear in the following pages.

Timeline

1655	Francis Nicholson born
1685	Daniel Dulany born
1689	Protestant Revolution in Maryland
1696	Annapolis becomes capital of Maryland
1697	Patrick Creagh born
1702–13	Queen Anne's War
1712	Jonas Green born
1715	Maryland returned to Baltimore proprietors
1728	Francis Nicholson dies
1736	Mary Chew (Paca) born
1737	Charles Carroll of Carrollton born
1739	War of Jenkins' Ear
1740	William Paca born
1741	Samuel Chase born
1744–48	King George's War
1745	John Shaw born
1753	Daniel Dulany dies
1755	Dr. Charles Carroll dies
1756–63	French and Indian War
1760	Patrick Creagh dies
1765	Stamp Act
1767	Jonas Green dies
1766–67	Paca House complete
1774	Mary Paca dies
1774	First Continental Congress
1775	Anne Catherine Green dies
1775–83	American Revolution
1786	Annapolis Convention
1787	U.S. Constitution
1789–97	George Washington president
1799	William Paca dies
1801–09	Thomas Jefferson president
1811	Samuel Chase dies
1829	John Shaw dies
1832	Charles Carroll of Carrollton dies

Builders of Annapolis

Portrait thought to be of Francis Nicholson, circa 1710. The portrait is now lost; the image used here is from a photograph probably provided by the dealer in 1940 when the painting was offered to the restorers of Colonial Willamsburg. Documentation on the search to authenticate the portrait is maintained in the reference files of the Maryland State Archives, Commission on Artistic Property. *(Photograph courtesy Maryland State Archives SC 1621-590. Curatorial note courtesy Carol Borchert, Maryland State Archives.)*

1

Governor Nicholson
Plans His Capital

On the eve of England's Glorious Revolution of 1688–89, Parliament was concerned that the greater threat to English liberties and representative government was not the crown but the army. A committee of the House of Commons fretted that "in the army it has grown into a principle that Parliaments are roots of rebellion, and Magna Carta sprung out of them." Oliver Cromwell, founder of the modern army, was said to have expressed the army's disdain more pithily: "Magna Carta, Magna F . . . ta."

The social and political attitudes of the army officer corps were shaped by service in garrison towns — in England, in Ireland, and on the coast of Africa. With the sole mission of maintaining law and order, commanders in these towns were exempted from the judicial process and were subject only to the king's martial law. After the Restoration of the Stuart monarchy in 1660, Charles II and his brother James II increasingly turned to military leaders for aid in keeping an unruly populace under control.

From the viewpoint of the king, the need to restore royal authority after 1660 was most evident in North America, where the colonies from Massachusetts to Carolina had slid, slowly but quite perceptibly, into virtual self-government. The Stuart kings countered this trend by filling the post of royal governor in each colony with soldiers, men whose sole loyalty was to the crown. The revolution of 1688–89,

which brought the Dutchman William of Orange and his wife Mary (one of the Protestant daughters of James II) to the throne of England, did nothing to blunt this policy. William in fact carried it further by revoking the proprietary charters of the Penn family in Pennsylvania and the Calvert family in Maryland and imposing royal governors of his own choosing. Between 1660 and 1720 more than 60 per cent of royal governors in British America were career army officers.

Francis Nicholson, whose service in America spanned a period of thirty-seven years and involved five different colonies, was perhaps the ablest of these soldier autocrats. Nicholson combined an authoritarian temperament (which at times raged out of control) with a genuine talent for leadership and the management of people. He had more impact on colonial American development than any other royal servant of his time.

We know little of Nicholson's youth and nothing of his parentage. He was born in 1655 at Downholme Parke, near Richmond in Yorkshire on part of the vast estate of the Duke of Bolton. He may have been a natural son of the duke, but, whether that was the case or not, the duke took an active interest in him and remained a valuable patron throughout his early career. Young Nicholson became a page to the duke's wife, and he grew up in an atmosphere of noble gentility. The training instilled a respect for authority, a love of order, and a *noblesse oblige* that measured social prominence by acts of philanthropy. This latter trait would be of great benefit to frontier America. In his public career Nicholson donated more funds to religion and learning than any other royal official in colonial America.

Despite the gentlemanly polish, he was without lands or lineage, and that limited his prospects in seventeenth-century England. Accordingly, he joined the army, enlisting in Charles II's Holland Regiment as an ensign in January 1678. The regiment had been sent to the Netherlands to aid the Dutch in their never ending struggle against the imperial appetites of France's King Louis XIV. Two years later, having advanced to lieutenant, he joined the newly raised "King's Own" Tangier regiment. Tangier (located at the western end of the Strait of Gibraltar), at

4

one time a Portuguese colony, had come into English hands as part of the dowry of Catherine of Braganza, who married Charles II in order to seal an alliance between England and Portugal. England's first outpost in Africa, Tangier was viewed as "the foundation of a new empire." However, it required a garrison of 3,000 men, and in the end it proved too much of a financial burden for the ever-strapped king.

Isolated and under siege by a Moroccan army, the Tangier garrison ruled by martial law. Percy Kirke, colonel of the Tangier Regiment, put to death anyone who disobeyed him. He found a kindred spirit in Lieutenant Nicholson and made him his envoy to the Emperor of Morocco. The Emperor's "Court of Fez" was, for Nicholson, another education in the art of despotism. Kirke also employed Nicholson as a messenger to carry dispatches to London. He made several remarkable rides across Spain and France, the last in the winter of 1683–84 when he (now a brevet captain) bore the news that the army was evacuating Tangier.

King Charles died the following year, and his successor, James II, determined to bring the obstreperous New England colonies (virtually self-governing under their corporate charters) under royal control. He created the Dominion of New England as an umbrella administration for the New England colonies. A short time later he added to the dominion his personal fiefdoms, the proprietary colonies of New York and New Jersey. To the post of "Captain-General and Governor in Chief" of the dominion the King named a professional soldier, Sir Edmund Andros. The dual purpose of the dominion was unified defense against the French and greater royal supervision of the empire. Both objectives required additional troops. The reinforcements included a company commanded by Captain Nicholson, who sailed across the Atlantic in midwinter 1686–87. Headquartered in Boston, Andros found Nicholson a valuable messenger for communicating the government's new policies to the isolated farmers of the interior. Nicholson undertook a series of arduous tours of the frontier, everywhere conveying the same message: "I ordered them to gett in their harvest, goeing to gether and taking a few of the Soldiers with them. . . . I told them that they must nott quit the place, for now they were happy under the protection of a greate King who protects all his Subjects both in their lifes and fortunes."

In July 1688 the Secretary for War and Colonies appointed Nicholson lieutenant governor of the dominion in charge of supervising the provinces of New York and New Jersey. Arriving in Manhattan, he found himself resented as the most recent of those governors "who had in a most arbitrary way subverted our ancient privileges making us in effect slaves to their will." Whether under English or Dutch rule, New Yorkers had never had much in the way of "privileges," but the attempt to remind leaders of their historic "rights" revealed a new spirit abroad in America. Unable to sense the change in popular temper, Nicholson tactlessly reminded the residents, English and Dutch alike, that they were "a conquered people" and therefore had no claim to the rights and privileges of Englishmen. They were subject to the will of the Crown, as expressed by its servant, the governor.

In the meantime, James II was attempting to govern England in the same highhanded way. His autocratic methods, together with his open adherence to the Roman Catholic faith, provoked a bloodless revolution that sent James scampering to France and brought William and Mary to the throne of England. News of William's landing in England reached Boston in April 1689, and a mob promptly slapped Governor Andros in jail. Word of the Boston uprising reached New York on April 26, and Nicholson quickly lost control. He might have saved his position and prevented an uprising (known as Leisler's Rebellion) if he had pledged allegiance to William and Mary and made some soothing statements about "rights" and "privileges." Instead, he called upon the army to suppress the growing disorder. When the Dutch-dominated militia refused to respond, he threatened to burn the city (as the British had done to Tangier when they evacuated). That cost him whatever support he might have had among the city's merchants, and Nicholson fled to the nearest ship to avoid arrest.

The change in sovereigns posed no threat to Nicholson's imperial career, for William's ministers adopted the Stuart policy of employing professional soldiers in the imperial service. With aid from his patron, the Duke of Bolton, Nicholson was given a new job as lieutenant governor of Virginia. (Because the titular governor never went to Virginia, Nicholson was in fact the chief executive of the province.) He arrived in May 1690 and found himself the only royal governor in America. He immediately sent home detailed plans for the restoration of imperial control in the colonies. Authorities in London were impressed enough to promote him to colonel.

Despite the posture he assumed in his communications with the New York populace, Nicholson seems to have learned something from the experience. He avoided the usual challenge to colonial rights, which in Virginia was an even more sensitive topic than in New York, and concentrated instead on some limited goals. He found Virginians, especially the common sort, an insecure people, living in fear of the twin bogeys of Catholic plots and Indian raids. He promptly undertook dramatic tours of the frontier where he reorganized the militia and instigated contests of running, riding, and shooting for rural youth. He brought government to the people in a way never done before. And the political results were soon evident. When he asked the assembly for troops for the defense of the frontier, the Assembly not only raised the force but authorized the Governor and Council to take any military action they chose. Nicholson wisely did not take advantage of the carte blanche, but he did note for the benefit of the Secretary for War and Colonies that he had met the Assembly and "I not only baffled them, but got things past contrary to their Interest."

In all of this Nicholson never lost sight of his basic mission, the preservation and extension of royal authority in America. He increased the crown's revenues by strictly enforcing the laws governing the tobacco trade. This made enemies of the planter-grandees on the royally appointed Governor's Council, but the discomfort of the Council oligarchy delighted the House of Burgesses, which was elected by the lesser planters and yeoman farmers. When the Council complained to the King about Nicholson's "Arbitrary and Imperious" behavior, the House of Burgesses voted him £300 for his services to Virginia and petitioned the Crown to allow him to accept it.

Nicholson also befriended the Reverend James Blair, named by the Bishop of London as commissary (head) of the Anglican Church in Virginia. Nicholson was a firm believer in the concept of church and state as close allies in the search for order, mutually dependent upon one another. He endorsed Blair's idea of a college in Virginia, named after the king and queen and supported by the church, because it would further both God's glory and His Majesty's interest. When the College of William and Mary was chartered in 1696 (after Nicholson had left the colony), he was named rector of the college and chair of the governing board. All in all, Nicholson's first tenure as governor of Virginia (he would later have a second, less successful term) was the most successful administration of his career.

In February 1692 Nicholson was appointed lieutenant governor of Maryland, newly made into a royal colony after the revocation of the proprietary charter. He made a tentative visit to his new domain, but upon learning that his enemy, Sir Edmund Andros (each had blamed the other for the fiasco of 1689), had been named the new governor of Virginia, he returned fuming to England. Nicholson remained in London for two years, spending much of his time working for the incorporation of the College of William and Mary. Although there is no evidence that he met with the celebrated architect Sir Christopher Wren at this time, it seems likely that he was instrumental in employing Wren to design the central building of the college. Wren and the urban planner John Evelyn were close associates, and, although there is likewise no evidence of contact between Nicholson and Evelyn, it is likely that both Evelyn and Wren had a profound influence on the plan for Nicholson's new capital, Annapolis. When he returned to Maryland in July 1694, he carried with him a copy of Evelyn's book on landscape planning.

Both Wren and Evelyn were heavily influenced by the baroque, a style, form, and mood that pervaded European architecture, painting, and music in the late seventeenth century. Turning away from the classical precision that marked the high Renaissance, baroque architecture employed curves and planes, seeking a perception of depth, for instance, by the setback of the wings of buildings from the central hall. The baroque period coincided with an era of city planning as the kings and princes of Europe sought to express their wealth and cultural advancement in the beauty and magnificence of their capital cities. They needed broad and straight avenues for their grand horse-drawn coaches, as well as for their great military parades. Andre Lenotre, who laid out Paris's Champs Élysées in 1670, was an apostle for a new landscape architecture featuring circles with axial patterns that focused on a point of climax. The Versailles and Tuileries Gardens, both of which reflected his influence, became models for urban planning across Europe.

The Great Fire of London, which gutted the city in 1666, provided both Wren and Evelyn an opportunity to remake a city that had emerged from the Middle Ages haphazardly, without plan or design. Each of them created a grand street plan, with avenues radiating from the more important cathedrals and public buildings, superimposed upon a grid of streets whose intersections often became circles and ovals for parks and statues. The plans were never adopted, although Wren, commissioned to rebuild St. Paul's Cathedral, produced a baroque masterpiece. Through their writings Wren and Evelyn nevertheless had an enormous impact on English landscape design.

The book by Evelyn that Nicholson acquired during his stay in London was *Sylva, or a Discourse of Forest Trees*. In planning the grounds for a manorial estate Evelyn proposed that

> Walks should not terminate abruptly, but rather in some capacious, or pretty figure, be in Circle, Oval, Semi-Circle, Triangle, or Square, especially in Parks, or where they do not lead into other Walks; and even in that case, that there may gracefully be a Circle to receive them.

Among the geometric figures available, Evelyn indicated his own preference was for "the Circle with a Star of Walks radiating from it," a result that he felt would be "exceeding pleasant."

The siting of a new capital for the province of Maryland had been the in the planning stage for some years. St. Mary's City had been the seat of government since the first settlers landed in 1634, but it had never amounted to much. The tobacco trade and the omnipresence of Chesapeake Bay retarded the growth of towns, despite the Calverts' best efforts to encourage the growth of New World metropolises. In 1668, on instructions from his father, the lord proprietor, Governor Cecil Calvert issued a proclamation establishing eleven town sites through which trade would be channeled. Ten years later St. Mary's was the only one that could be located on a map. "But it can hardly be called a town," Cecil Calvert explained to the Lords of Trade and Plantations, "being in length . . . about five miles, and in breadth . . . not above one mile, in all which space, excepting only my own house and buildings wherein the said courts and public offices are kept, there are not above thirty houses, and those at considerable distances from each other."

There were other reasons as well for moving. Population had moved westward up the Potomac and northward along the shores of Chesapeake Bay in the sixty years since the colony was founded. St. Mary's was an inconvenient meeting place for courts and legislature. Recognizing this, Governor Calvert summoned the General Assembly in October 1683 to meet at the house of a planter in Anne Arundel County (the county was named for the wife of Cecil Calvert, second Lord Baltimore). At his urging the Assembly designated thirty-one town sites throughout the province and appointed commissioners in each to survey the lots. Two of the most centrally located sites were in Anne Arundel County — one on the South River (later named London Town), the other near the mouth of the Severn River.

The site on the Severn River had initially been settled by a group of Puritans who had been expelled from Virginia in 1648. They laid out a town on the north bank near Greenbury Point and named it Providence. Other members of the group moved across the river and settled near the mouth of Spa Creek (called Carroll's Creek through the first century of Annapolis's history). The community was known as Proctor's Landing until the creation of Anne Arundel County in 1650; thereafter it was usually referred to as Anne Arundel Town or Arundelton. In 1684 the Assembly passed an act creating "Anne Arundel Town" on a hundred acres of land donated by Robert Proctor and the proprietor. The county surveyor, Richard Beard, was ordered to survey a street plan. Beginning at the foot of what later became Duke of Gloucester Street near Proctor's tavern, Beard drew straight lines for the principal streets, a grid of cross streets, and he staked out some lots. However, no settlers arrived, and Proctor died, leaving his widow as the sole inhabitant. Governor Calvert actually favored the South River site for the new capital, but all plans for the relocation of the seat of government were scrapped when he returned to England in 1684.

The Revolution of 1689 revived the urge to relocate the capital. Maryland had been founded as a Catholic refuge, and although Protestants soon outnumbered Catholics in the population, the Catholic element remained strong in St. Mary's County. Protestants supported the change to a royal colony in 1689, and they were eager to move the government out of the area of Catholic influence.

When Nicholson called his first meeting of the Maryland Assembly in September 1694, the principal order of business was the establishment of a new seat of government. The Assembly passed two bills, which received the governor's signature in October. The first was a town authorization act of the sort that the Assembly had been enacting for some years. It provided for the establishment of two new communities to be laid out on land acquired by purchase or by eminent domain. Each would be a port of entry to the colony. One was Oxford in Talbot County on the Eastern Shore, and the other was to be located on "the Land Called the Town Land att Seavern in Ann Arundel County where the Town was formerly." This suggests that Arundelton, which had been indicated on maps of the Chesapeake as recently as 1683, had been abandoned. As a result, the commissioners appointed to supervise the planning would have little difficulty in acquiring the land and following the act's instructions to "Cause the same to be marked Staked and Divided into Convenient Streets, lanes and Alleys with other spare places to be left on which may be a Church Chapell, Market House or other publick building." The act further specified that in Anne Arundel town (but, significantly, not Oxford) the commissioners were to acquire a substantial area "adjoyning in or near to the Town Land . . . to be fenced in and Called the Town Common or Pasture." The Assembly clearly envisioned future urban growth for the community on the Severn.

The other law was more controversial because it provoked the violent opposition of the inhabitants of St. Mary's. It designated "Arrundel Town" as "the Chief place and Seat of Justice within the Province for holding of Assemblys and Provinciall Courts." Anticipating opposition, the assembly wrote its rationale into the law. Religion was not mentioned. Instead, the statute stressed the inconvenience suffered by persons who had to make a long journey to attend the courts or the legislature. One consequence was that criminals often escaped justice because witnesses refused to undergo such hardship merely to give testimony. The statute then went on to direct the town commissioners "to survey and lay out in the most commodious and convenient part and place of the said Towne six Acres of Land intire for the erecting a Court House and other buildings as shall be thought necessary and convenient." The act specified in considerable detail the dimensions, design, and materials to be used in the capitol (State House) building. The lower floor was to be laid in brick, the upper floors in planking, and the roof to be shingled with cypress. Unfortunately the first structure proved to be too combustible. It burned to the ground in 1704 and had to be replaced.

As expected, the inhabitants of St. Mary's denounced the act, and, in a bid to retain the seat of government, they offered to finance a daily "coach or caravan" from the Assembly hall in St. Mary's to the Patuxent River, as well as a dozen horses for persons "having occasion to ride post, or otherwise, with or without a guide, to any port of the province on the Western Shore." Nicholson referred the petition to the Assembly, which dismissed it with contemptuous sarcasm.

The following year the Assembly gave the capitol a dual mission of serving as courthouse for Anne Arundel County, an arrangement that continued until 1769. One room in the building was set aside for the town clerk of Annapolis (the name conferred on the town in honor of Princess Anne, James's other Protestant daughter, who would come to the throne on the death of King William in 1702).

The original plan for the city of Annapolis was lost when the State House burned in 1704. A survey map of 1718, indicating street names and numbered lots, has likewise been lost. We have today only a copy of that map, made in 1743. The illustration in this book is a 1956 copy that provides more legibly the names of streets and lot owners. Because the historical record is so sparse, the evidence that Nicholson authored the plan is purely circumstantial. Nevertheless, it seems a good bet, based on his familiarity with the work of Wren and Evelyn, and the fact that he took the trouble to bring to Maryland one of Evelyn's sketchbooks. Moreover, there is no evidence that anyone else authored the plan, and it is highly unlikely that a colonial land surveyor would have conceived such an intricate scheme, especially one based on a baroque formula. Other Maryland towns built about this time — Chester Town is a good example — were laid out on an uninterrupted grid pattern. Nicholson may have had help, but the inspiration was clearly his.

Dominating the neck of land between the arc of what is now College Creek and the Severn River was a small knoll, about three hundred yards from the natural inlet that would serve as the town's harbor. Nicholson designated that as the site for the new State House. He defined the site by drawing a circle around the base of the knoll, 520 feet in diameter. To the west of this State House circle, separated from it by a slight dip in the land, was another elevation. Around this Nicholson drew another, somewhat smaller, circle as the site for an Anglican church.

Balancing the two circles, Nicholson drew two squares, although the size and placement of the squares hardly gives a sense of balance. The larger one, 360 feet on a side, lay to the north of State House circle, and a corner of it abutted on church circle. Twelve residential lots formed the borders of this square, leaving a square of open space in the middle. Streets penetrated between the lots to the interior park from the midpoint of each side of the square. The concept dated back to city planners of the Renaissance, and it was being extensively employed in the rebuilding of London. Bloomsbury Square in London had recently become a fashionable residential address; by

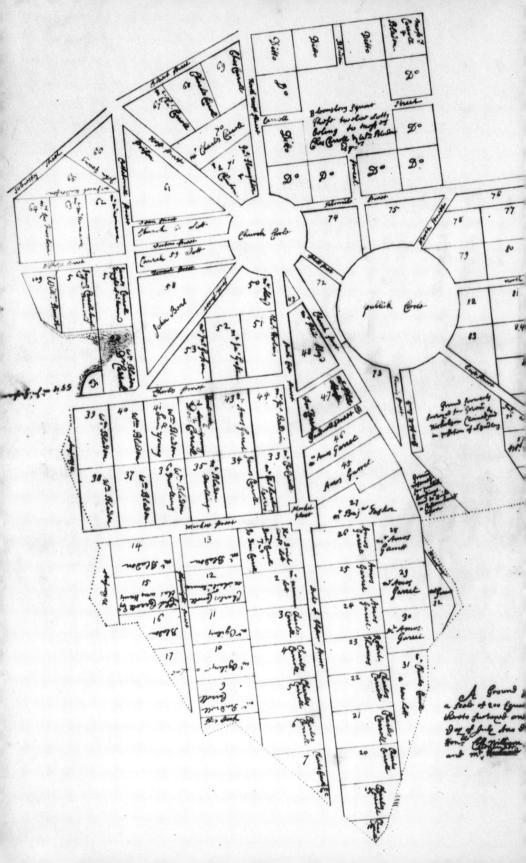

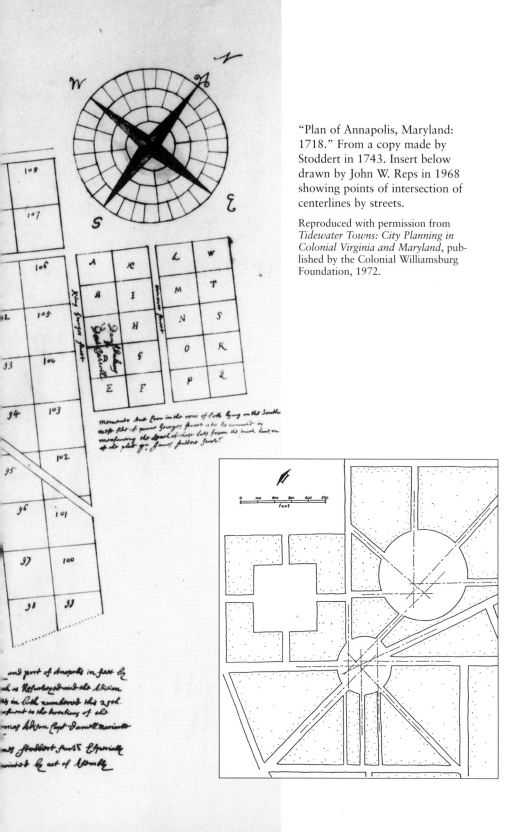

"Plan of Annapolis, Maryland: 1718." From a copy made by Stoddert in 1743. Insert below drawn by John W. Reps in 1968 showing points of intersection of centerlines by streets.

Reproduced with permission from *Tidewater Towns: City Planning in Colonial Virginia and Maryland*, published by the Colonial Williamsburg Foundation, 1972.

appropriating the name, Nicholson clearly hoped to achieve a similar result in Annapolis.

The other, much smaller, square was placed at the midpoint of a street (later named Duke of Gloucester Street) that emanated from the church circle and ran to Carroll's (Spa) Creek. Nicholson labeled this location Market Square, though it would appear to be an odd location for a city market. It was not near the harbor and was not located on any axis between points of interest, such as the harbor, the State House, or the church. Perhaps Nicholson had in mind the injunction in the statute creating Annapolis that trades which were considered a neighborhood nuisance —"Baker Brewer Tanner Dyer"—be placed "a sufficient distance" from the residential community. The square is still evident on the plat of 1718, though whether it was still functioning as a market is uncertain, since the center of commercial activity remained at the harbor. (The site is occupied by City Hall today, and the only remnant is Market Street running southwest to Spa Creek.) Between the Market and Carroll's Creek Nicholson seems to have followed the survey originally done by Richard Beard in 1683. Beard was still in the colony, and, at the Assembly's request, he executed a new survey and map in 1695. Nicholson incorporated it into his own plan, and as a result Gloucester, Shipwright, and Market Streets correspond to streets surveyed by Beard.

Radiating from the two circles were avenues in the baroque mode, each named by the direction in which it ran, except for Church Street (Main Street today), which ran from the church circle to the harbor. Joining the two circles was a thin avenue named School Street. The name was probably derived from the proximity to State House circle of King William's School, chartered in 1696 with Nicholson as one of its trustees. This school was the only tangible result of a system of public schools, one in each county, that Nicholson had proposed to the legislature in 1694. King William's School owed its existence, in large measure, to the fact that Nicholson donated one of his own town lots for the site of a building, paid a contractor £10 to erect a brick schoolhouse, and personally subscribed £50 toward its endowment.

Aside from the fact that it is unique, the most striking peculiarity of the Annapolis street plan is the apparent errors in design. One feature that literally springs from the map is the incoherence of street center-lines. If one drew an extension of the centerline of each street entering one of the two circles, the lines would not intersect at the center of the circles or at any other common point. For example, if West Street and East Street were extended into the State House circle, they would never meet. And School Street, the interim avenue between the two, would not connect with either (other than by crossing them at an angle). In short, the "radial" avenues are not radial at all because there is no focal point, as envisioned by the baroque designers. Another flaw is that School Street is far too narrow for its function of calling atten-tion to the two edifices at each end. Francis Street, leading from the State House circle to the harbor, is also a curiously weak link between the city landing and its governmental *raison d' être*. A professional European planner would have corrected all these errors. That Nicholson did not — and apparently did not even spot them — sug-gests that he failed to fully appreciate the objectives of baroque street design. He was, after all, an amateur in city planning. He may have confined himself to a hasty sketch and left the details to others. Because Annapolis "streets" remained nothing more than dirt paths for more than a century, it is likely that no one noticed.

Construction of the State House began in the spring of 1696, although completion was delayed due to lack of funds and the lack-adaisical performance of its builder, Colonel Casparus Herman. In the meantime the legislature met in a hastily built frame structure on College Creek provided by Colonel Edward Dorsey, who owned much of the land on which the town was built. Some, though probably not all, members of the legislature (there were forty-two members of the lower house and twelve councilors) were housed at the inn of Rachel Proctor, Robert's widow.

The legislature apparently did not take possession of the capitol until 1698, by which time there was considerable grumbling over the cost of Nicholson's elaborate plan for the city. The new facility did not improve legislative tempers. The General Assembly and the govern-ment clerks shared the same building, and to get to their offices the clerks had to pass through the Assembly's meeting room. When it was dealing with sensitive matters, the Assembly barred its doors, which left the clerks outside in the cold or imprisoned in their offices.

Nicholson's tactlessness turned an inconvenient situation into a mini-crisis. Taking advantage of the fact that the capitol was also used as an Anglican church, on Sunday, May 6, Nicholson posted a notice on the door of the building stating that the clerks must have access to their offices at all times. When the legislature returned the next day, it reacted angrily. "This house does highly resent and are much grieved to see their privileges so much entrenched upon," it wrote the governor. It went on to point out that it had attempted to accommodate the clerks and interfered with their passageway only when "our duty to his Majesty's service required." Nicholson replied that he had not intended to encroach upon the privileges of the house and that he had posted the notice on a Sunday so it would come to the attention of the general public. He then poured new fuel on the fire by reminding the legislators that the colony was on the brink of insolvency and there was much work to be done. He suggested that the legislature, rather than fretting about its privileges, might economize by reducing its own size.

Rather than wait for a rejoinder, Nicholson sent the assembly home for a day — a gentle reminder that he could dissolve it altogether if it became too obstreperous. Then, at last, he displayed some leadership. He invited key legislators to dinner that evening and somehow managed to defuse the crisis. When the Assembly returned the next day, it dropped the subject of accommodations and turned its attention to the colony's mounting debts.

The capitol was damaged by a lightning bolt the following year. After it was destroyed completely by fire in 1704, a second capitol — this time of brick — was quickly put together. A visitor described this building as

> An oblong square in form, the entrance hall opposite which, two or three steps from the floor, was the judges' seat, and on each side were apartments used as jury rooms. . . . On the upper floor were three

apartments, the two largest were used for the Upper and Lower House of Assembly and the other was the apartment for the mace-bearer and other officers depending thereon.

This structure served the colony until 1770, when it was demolished for lack of size, and replaced by the present capitol.

The Anglican Church, aptly named after Saint Anne, was also begun in 1696. Parish records have been lost, so its source of funding is unknown. Nicholson almost certainly was one of its sponsors since the Church of England was the principal beneficiary of his lifetime of philanthropy. (The Anglican Church, together with the Society for the Propagation of the Gospel, received a munificent total of £2,150 sterling in gifts from Nicholson.) Construction was nevertheless delayed, perhaps because of Nicholson's departure from the colony, and it was still unfinished when the parishioners began meeting there eight years later. Like the State House, the church underwent a number of fires and demolitions. The present structure dates from 1859.

In the original plan a parallelogram of land, bounded by East Street, Francis Street, State House circle, and the dock, was reserved for the governor himself. This was the "common" or "public pasture" mentioned in the city's enabling act of 1696. On this tract Nicholson constructed a house for himself, situated on what is now the corner of Cornhill and Hyde streets. Both of these narrow carriageways were cut through the common land in the eighteenth century to permit its subdivision into small residential lots. Below the governor's residence the commons between Prince George Street and the harbor was set aside, on Nicholson's orders, for a "ship carpenter's lot." A visitor in 1699 described the new town.

> Governour Nicholson has done his endeavor to make a town. . . . There are in itt about forty dwelling houses, of seven of eight whereof cann afford good lodging and accomodations for strangers. There is alsoe a State House and a free schoole built with bricke which make a great shew among a parcell of wooden houses, and a foundation of a church laid, the only bricke church in Maryland. They have two market daies in the week, and had Governour Nicholson continued there some years longer he had brought it to some perfection.

In 1698 the decision-makers in London promoted Nicholson to the governorship of the larger and wealthier colony of Virginia. He had had a successful tour in Maryland, providing the most honest and effective leadership that the colony had experienced in sixty-five years of existence. He worked remarkably well with the Assembly, holding elections on schedule and calling legislators into session more frequently than any of his Calvert predecessors. Although he was dedicated, as he told his first Assembly, to the causes of "Religion, Service of the King & Interest of the Countrey," he avoided an open battle over popular "rights" and "privileges." When he asked for a bill making the Church of England the established church in Maryland, the Assembly insisted on tacking on language to the effect that "Justice shall be administered according to the Laws of England." Nicholson capitulated, explaining to the Secretary for War and Colonies that it was impossible to get the act "without some Clause about Liberty and property which your Grace very well knows Englishmen are fond of."

During his last years in Maryland Nicholson faced some strident opposition from chronic malcontents backed by the Catholic population of St. Mary's. He jailed some of the leaders when they became too clamorous but otherwise tolerated the dissent. He departed the colony on January 2, 1698/99, genuinely popular among the citizenry and with a eulogy from the Assembly ringing in his ears. His new-found maturity as a colonial administrator was expressed in a letter a few months later to the Board of Trade, an agency created by King William to manage colonial affairs. He advised the board to screen candidates for governor very carefully because in the future it would be essential that any governor "be esteemed by the people, or at least the major part of them, to be a lover of them and their Country, and not that he be Sent or comes to make or retrieve a fortune."

His second term in Virginia started out well enough. He eventually ran into trouble principally because the political opposition (Whigs) was better organized and more principled than it had been in Maryland. Nicholson began by cooperating with his old ally Commissary James Blair, who wanted to move the seat of government out of low-lying, pestilential Jamestown. Nicholson himself probably drafted the act of 1699 that created the town of Williamsburg, where the College of William and Mary had already been sited. The act laid out the streets and specified the plans for the capitol building, an austere, though faintly baroque structure in the shape of an "H" with rounded turrets at the four corners. The centerpiece of the street plan was a broad, mile-long avenue (The Duke of Gloucester Street) that connected the two dominant structures of the town, the college and the capitol, with Bruton Parish Church abutting the street about halfway between the two. It was a simpler plan than that for Annapolis, and in some ways more elegant.

The Virginia Assembly readily appropriated funds for the construction of the capitol building, but it balked when Nicholson asked for an appropriation to build a suitable residence for the governor. The most he could obtain was authority to purchase sixty acres of land on the northern edge of the grid of streets. (The Palace Green today connects the tract to The Duke of Gloucester Street.) Nicholson left the colony before any work was started on his residence.

Nicholson's difficulty in obtaining an appropriation for a residence was part of a political contest that had developed between the governor and the Council. This, in turn, involved the larger constitutional issue of executive versus legislative power. Nicholson's war with the Council, which also functioned as the upper house of the legislature, foreshadowed the later imperial contests between royal governors and colonial assemblies that ultimately led to the American Revolution. Since James Blair was the leading figure on the Council, the struggle became a highly personal one, exacerbated by Nicholson's evil temper, a character trait that he had somehow suppressed while serving in Maryland. Blair ultimately sailed for England to lobby for Nicholson's removal. Blair succeeded when the Tories, who had been favored by Queen Anne, fell from power and were replaced by a Whig ministry headed by the Duke of Marlborough, hero of the Battle of Blenheim. Marlborough wanted to reward his own lieutenants with colonial posts, and Colonel Alexander Spottswood replaced Nicholson in Virginia in 1705.

The war with France and Spain ("The War of the Spanish

Succession") that had begun in 1702 spread to America in 1709 when Nicholson was given command of an expedition to conquer Canada. The expedition, which was to descend on Montreal by way of Lake Champlain, never materialized, but the following year, 1710, Nicholson commanded an amphibious operation that seized Nova Scotia from the French. By this time he held the rank of lieutenant general and the title "Governor of Governors," with authority over all civil governors in matters of troops and army supplies. Endowed with such heady power, Nicholson regressed to the character training of his youth. He and his army treated the poor, French-speaking inhabitants of Acadia as if the place were another Tangier. His temper became more and more out of control. After watching one of his demented rages, an Indian ally observed that the general was "born drunk."

The end of the war in 1714 and Queen Anne's death a year later (she was succeeded by a German prince, George I), suspended for a time Nicholson's military and administrative career. Although he was more than sixty years old, he remained, nevertheless, in the thoughts of the Board of Trade. In 1719, the people of South Carolina, tired of a proprietary regime that seemed incapable of defending the colony against Indians, pirates, and the Spanish in Florida, asked the crown to take possession of it as a royal colony. The king obliged, and the Board of Trade sent Nicholson to the colony as its first royal governor. In the colony he revived the familiar program of reorganizing the militia, endowing churches, engaging the frontiersmen, and plucking the tail feathers of the planter élite. He turned seventy in 1725 and decided it was time to retire. He returned to London and died just three years later. He never quite succeeded in his lifetime goal of rendering the colonies efficient, profitable, and submissive partners in the British Empire, but no royal official of his time left a greater imprint on the dawning civilization that was America.

2

Patrick Creagh,
Self-Made Entrepreneur

What first struck travelers who visited colonial America was that there were no monuments and no ruins. In Britain one could hardly travel a day's journey without chancing upon a stone circle erected by Druids, a road laid out by Romans, or a castle built by some medieval baron. In America there was nothing like this. All was new. And when anything became worn out, it was usually torn down and replaced. America had no past; it was a land without history. The newness conditioned its people. Having cast aside much of the cultural baggage brought over from Europe, they were inventive, inquisitive, open to new ideas and new ways of doing things. They were free without having, as yet, a philosophy of freedom.

In this fluid society, versatility and inventiveness often yielded higher rewards than formal training and professionalism. In America the jack of all trades, self-made and self-reliant, has always been held in higher regard than the learned professor; practical results are held in higher esteem than abstract theories. We sometimes think of Benjamin Franklin as one of the leading scientists of the eighteenth century because of his experiments with electricity. Yet look at his inventions: the lightning rod, the rocking chair, and the enclosed stove — all symbols of the American concern for practical results. Franklin was the preeminent jack of all trades, the prototype for all others. The subject of this chapter is Maryland's counterpart to Philadelphia's Franklin, Patrick Creagh.

Patrick Creagh was born on the Eastern Shore, probably in Kent County in 1697. His grandfather, James Creagh, had migrated from England some years before, probably as a mariner. When James Creagh died in 1703 he left an estate of a little less than 5 pounds, consisting almost entirely of carpenters tools and navigation instruments. Patrick Creagh, Sr. was a struggling Kent County merchant, constantly hauled into court by London agents for failing to remit enough tobacco to pay for the goods he had ordered. The final court summons was levied in 1716 against his widow Mary, who by then had moved with her son to Annapolis. When Mary died two years later, she left an estate of 8 pounds, 10 shillings.

Patrick Creagh burst upon the stage of history, seemingly from a standing start, on March 11, 1730, when he unfolded 190 pounds of current money of Maryland for the purchase of three lots, 95, 98, and 99 on Prince George Street, Annapolis. The deed was not recorded until 1735, apparently because several of the former owners resided in London, and by that date he had almost certainly begun to build the house which stands today on lot 95. By then, too, he was married and widowed, and left with two children, James and Elizabeth. Some time after 1735 he again married, to Frances Smith, but they would have no more children. He left the house to her by his will, drafted in 1747 (the first record we have of the house).

By this time he was well-established as a merchant, although his store, if indeed it was located outside of his house, has never been located. He had also begun to build ships, a craft inherited from his father and grandfather and schooled by the shipwrights and watermen of the Eastern Shore. The correlation between trade and shipbuilding was patent: a merchant greatly increased his profits when he could ship goods in his own bottoms. However, the combination was also highly unusual. Few merchants had any knowledge of shipbuilding, and few shipwrights accumulated enough capital to indulge in trade. One author counts Creagh and his Annapolis neighbors, Samuel

The Patrick Creagh House, or "Aunt Lucy's Bake Shop" on Prince George Street. *Photo by author.*

Galloway and Dr. Charles Carroll, as the only merchant-shipbuilders in the English colonies.

Creagh's boatworks lay on the sea oat–strewn beach at the foot of Prince George Street, a site given to the city by Governor Nicholson in 1719, to be used as a shipyard. On July 29, 1735, Creagh boldly petitioned the colony's land office for a slice of this ground:

> I desire you will enter in my name the Ship Carpenter's lot and the Small Slip of Ground adjoining thereto, lying on the South Side of Prince George Street, a sit is not yet improved, and on which I delight to improve, and you will oblige,

> Your Humble Servant, Pat Creagh.

The colony sold him the land, and a decade later he expanded his holding to the east, acquiring a tract of five and a half acres between Prince George Street and the water, patented in the land office books as "Creagh's Discovery."

Shipbuilding required a variety of skilled craftsmen: joiners, caulkers, coopers, glaziers, sailmakers, and the like. Where Creagh found these skills in rudimentary Annapolis we do not know. What we do know — from ads he placed in newspapers for the recovery of runaways — is that he used a substantial number of white bonded servants. These persons, who bound themselves to a period of service in return for their passage to America, sometimes possessed rudimentary training in a craft. Creagh may have scanned every incoming boatload for bonded workers.

Creagh's shipyard soon became the site of his first public works, a colony jail (spelled "gaol" or "goal" in the eighteenth century). The colonial Assembly itself commissioned him to build the jail and paid him £1,500 for the project in five installments, the first three in 1738 and the last two the following year. Where Creagh learned the craft of brickmason is not clear; perhaps he was self-taught. In any case, the structure lasted for forty years. It was pulled down after the Revolution, probably for lack of maintenance.

During these same years the Assembly commissioned him to construct a brick building on the east side of state circle to house the newly created Commissioners for Emitting Bills of Credit, i.e., the colony's paper money. The "Old Treasury" still stands, a fine testimonial to Creagh's artistry and craftsmanship. It also caught the governor's attention, for shortly after it was completed Governor Thomas Bladen approached Creagh with the idea of building a house suitable for the chief executive of the colony.

The contract the governor and "Patrick Creagh, Painter" (another self-taught craft?) signed on January 28, 1742, sited the structure "upon the hill behind Mr. Stephen Bordley's house where the Powder House formerly stood" (presently McDowell Hall of St. John's College). Creagh was to supply 400,000 good bricks by the last day of October in lots that would enable the Committee to inspect and

The Old Treasury on the State House lawn, built by Patrick Creagh, ca. 1737. It is the oldest existing government house in America. *Photo by M. E. Warren.*

approve them. He also undertook to deliver 6,000 bushels of clear good lime, made of the best seashells, at 8 pence a bushel. The "Publick" would pay £1,600 for the bricks in installments, as they were delivered, and £200 for the lime.

Creagh seems to have served as the equivalent of a modern-day general contractor on the project, obtaining the materials and equipment and employing the labor. On September 22, 1744, he sent a bill to the governor in the amount of 629 pounds, 12 shillings, 5 pence for the following items: pine planks, oak scantling, cartage fees for hauling thirty-five pieces of large framing, 2,445 bushels of lime, 220,000 bricks, and eleven days' work on the part of Creagh's mason. On October 3 he billed the governor for another 278 bushels of lime, and on January 9 for another 36,900 bricks, two days' work for his team hauling large timber, and cartage fees for twenty-nine bolts and spikes and fifty-three loads of nails. It would appear that Creagh did everything *except* paint the building.

Where did Creagh obtain this huge quantity of construction materials? One clue is a contract signed on May 22, 1742, with John Brice II, fellow merchant and Prince George Street neighbor (the "first Brice house," built in the early 1730s, is now 195 Prince George Street). By the agreement Creagh and Brice purchased Swan Neck, a tract of 250 acres on the north side of the Severn River, with timber and quarries. In November of that year, presumably after receiving the first installment of money under his contract with Governor Bladen, Creagh bought out Brice's half. Brice seems to have staked his neighbor, in effect, to this source of raw materials.

As construction went on, the Assembly, which had appropriated £4,000 for the structure in 1742, became increasingly distressed at the size and cost of the governor's project. It refused to make any further appropriation for Creagh's bills for the year 1744, and Creagh apparently quit work on the project. Townspeople dubbed the empty hulk, left open to wind and rain, "Bladen's Folly." In the meantime, Stephen Bordley, one of the leaders of the antiproprietary (or "country") faction in the lower house, further muddied the situation by serving notice that the four-acre lot on which Bladen was building belonged to him. Bordley's claim was ephemeral, resting on rights twice declared invalid by a colonial court. But it was enough to arouse Lord Baltimore, who sent a sharp reminder to Bladen to protect his "town lands." The controversy no doubt hastened Bladen's recall. Bordley, one of the town's more prosperous attorneys, threatened to take his case all the way to the king, but in the end he accepted the Assembly's offer of £200 to extinguish his claim.

In March 1747 Samuel Ogle landed in Maryland to replace Bladen as governor. To his credit, the inept Bladen remained in the colony and did his best to ensure that Creagh was treated fairly. In resubmitting Creagh's bills from 1744 for payment, Bladen attested: "I am persuaded the above amount is just but it is to be remembered that the sum of

£499 is due the Publick from Mr. Creagh by virtue of a contract with his present excellency Samuel Ogle, as can be made to appear."

By this time there was no chance that Creagh would ever be paid. Britain and France had gone to war in 1744, and the fighting had spread to North America where the colonial assemblies were expect-ed to supply men and money. Neither Governor Ogle nor the Assembly, both short of cash and ever more dependent on issues of paper money, was inclined to appropriate any additional funds for "Bladen's Folly." When Creagh's invoices for 1744 were resubmitted to the Assembly in 1747, the lower house named a committee to inves-tigate the project. Its report was devastating:

> Your Committee further find, That several Bricks in the new House erected on the said Land for the use of the Governor for the Time being, are moulter'd and Decayed; and that there is a Crack in the wall of said House from the Bottom almost to the Top, in the Northeast corner thereof; That there is Round the outside of the said House a Quantity of Portland Stone, Bremen Stone, several Casks of Stucco, and some wrought Country stone; That within the Cellars of Said House is a large Quantity of Shingles, which appear to lie on the bare Ground; and likewise some marble stone and Bremen Stone lying on the damp Ground, which last appear much Decayed; That there is a large Quantity of plank and scant-ling lying in Great Danger of being spoiled, occasioned by the Rains coming through the Roof of the House; and that part of the sommers of the said House appears to be upon decay; Jews-Ears growing now out of the sides thereof.

The committee's indictment gave the assembly an excuse to disallow any payment of the invoices. So far as is known, Creagh was never paid for his work on "Bladen's Folly." He survived nonetheless, and even prospered. The war, which had distracted the Assembly's atten-tion from civil works, ironically opened new avenues of trade and profit for Patrick Creagh.

The war began as a spat between Spain and Britain over trade in the Caribbean. Spain, as it had for centuries, sought to maintain a monop-oly over the wealth of its empire. It did this by confining trade between Spain and the Caribbean to an annual convoy of galleons, which disposed of their goods and refilled their holds with gold, silver, cocoa, and exotic hardwoods at giant "trade fairs" held at Pôrto Bello on the coast of Panama and Cartagena on the coast of present-day Columbia. The convoy system was self-defeating because, in the intervening months, British ship captains, with cheaper and better-made goods to sell, plied the coast of the Spanish main trading with local merchants. As the British interlopers grew in numbers, the convoys of Spanish galleons got smaller every year.

Spain combated the intrusion by chasing and seizing the interlopers. One British merchant captain, Edward Jenkins, was intercepted by a Spanish coast guard vessel, whose commander boarded his ship and punished him by cutting off his ear. Or so Jenkins claimed. In any case, he returned to England with a mysterious box and a story of Spanish treachery. He was an instant hit with the parliamentary opposition to the ministry of Robert Walpole, which had been hammering Walpole for his weakness toward Spain. Jenkins and his box appeared before a committee of the House of Commons, and within weeks the government declared war, a conflict known ever after as the War of Jenkins' Ear. It was from the beginning a political war (one cynic hinted that the occasion for the war would have been eliminated if someone in the Commons had asked Jenkins to take off his wig), a war begun without plan and without strategic objective.

Whenever England went to war with Spain, the memories of Englishmen turned to the glorious days of Queen Elizabeth and the daring raids of her "sea dogs" on the Spanish Main. In July 1739, three months before war was declared, Admiral Edward Vernon (a vocal member of Parliament who claimed he could conquer Pôrto Bello "with only six ships") was named fleet commander in the Caribbean and instructed "to destroy the Spanish settlements in the West Indies and to distress their shipping by every method whatever." On November 20, exactly one month after the declaration of war, he sailed from Jamaica with six line-of-battle ships. Pôrto Bello, unaware that a war had begun, was caught without a single gun in service. Vernon's sailors seized the castle with scarcely a shot fired, and the treasure port was in British hands.

England went mad with joy, and the ministry authorized a larger expedition of land and sea forces to proceed against Cartagena. This port was the depot for the export of Peruvian gold, made the more inviting as a target when it was learned that the galleon convoy of 1737 was still lying in the harbor.

More than any earlier contest, this was an imperial war, and the ministry decided that the colonies should lend a hand. During the winter letters went out to the colonial governors asking them to enlist men and gather supplies for the expedition. Maryland's governor, Samuel Ogle, laid his letter before the Council on April 11, 1740, and he issued a proclamation urging His Majesty's faithful servants to enlist upon the glorious enterprise. Promised that they would receive the same rank and pay as British regulars, as well as a share in the booty, several hundred Marylanders volunteered for service. The Assembly appropriated £5,000 to organize and outfit three companies of men. The colonies altogether supplied 3,600 men to the British attack force, placed under the command of Virginia's Governor William Gooch.

The colonies undertook to provision and transport their troops to the West Indies rendezvous (Jamaica), and in Maryland that responsibility fell upon the mercantile community of Annapolis. Patrick Creagh and his fellows, ever ready to blend patriotism with profit, performed it grandly. In September 1740, the assembly allocated 330 pounds, 5 shillings, 8 pence to Creagh "for maintaining on Shoar and finding House Room and firing [cooking fires] for 297 Men of his Majestys Forces." He received an additional £945 "for transporting 105 men Officers included being Captain John Lloyds Company and finding Necessaries on Board to the Place of General Rendezvous in the West Indies as by Charter Party date 30 August 1740." Creagh was also paid 2 pounds, five shillings for providing the cooperage and horses to carry 4,978 gallons of water for ships embarking from the Patuxent River. A bill of September 23, 1740, paid him 144 pounds for 48 barrels of pork, and in December he received another 416 pounds, 8 shillings for transporting another "Charter Party" to the "General Rendezvous."

Two of Patrick Creagh's vessels were employed as troop transports for the Cartagena expedition, and a third may have carried the pork

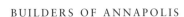

barrels and other foodstuffs. We do not know how many vessels Creagh owned at any one time, but the port records indicate that at one time or another between 1734 and 1749 he owned fourteen vessels. Two of these were ships (square-sail rigging and 100 to 200-tons displacement) of the sort used in the transatlantic tobacco trade. He had three vessels in the 50- to 100-ton range, rigged as brigs or snows (a mixture of square and triangular sails), and the rest were one- or two-masted sloops and schooners. These latter vessels, ranging from 20 to 50 tons, were used only in the intercolonial and West Indies trade. Their chief virtue was not carrying capacity but speed. The West Indies trade — interloping in the French and Spanish empires — required quickness, even in time of peace. From the nature of his fleet, then, it would seem that Creagh had been involved in the West Indies trade even before the outbreak of war.

The Cartagena expedition was a fiasco. Vernon sat in Jamaica through the fall and winter, fretting about a French squadron that was lurking about Haiti to the north, even though the British and French were not yet at war. During the delay his amphibious force was weakened by tropical diseases and the effects of Jamaican rum. ("Captain Punch" was alleged to be the most ferocious enemy Vernon's army saw.) His fleet finally arrived off the harbor of Cartagena on March 3, 1741, but Vernon delayed a week trying to decide where to land. This gave the garrison, already stronger than the British had anticipated, ample time to prepare. The final British assault, on April 9, was made against the strongest part of the city's fortifications, and when the grenadiers fought their way to the rampart, they found their scaling ladders were too short. Of the 6,600 men who had landed, only 3,000 returned to their ships on April 17.

The only unit in Vernon's army cited for gallantry was a contingent of two hundred Virginians commanded by Captain Lawrence Washington (elder half-brother of George). Washington's admiration for Vernon likewise survived the debacle, for he named his plantation on the bluffs overlooking the Potomac "Mount Vernon." The rest of the colonial force returned home with feelings of deep resentment. They had been mistreated by British officers, denied any share in the plunder (there was none in any case), and some were impressed for sea duty in the Royal Navy. It is a marvel that there were any volunteers at all three years later for an Anglo-American assault on French Canada.

Patrick Creagh nevertheless remained interested in the commercial potential of the West Indies. In 1740 fighting on the continent of Europe had broken out between Prussia and Austria. Britain and France were drawn in on opposite sides in 1744. American vessels, excluded from the French sugar islands in time of peace, found themselves welcomed in time of war. By exporting their goods in American bottoms, the French evaded the British blockade. Creagh's speedy sloops and schooners were ideal for this traffic. His success is evidenced by an advertisement in the *Maryland Gazette*, over his name, on August 23 1745:

> To Be Sold; By the Subscriber, good Barbados Rum, Muscavado Sugar, good large fresh lymes; also good French brandy by wholesale or retail. Likewise, good French claret and 2 likely young negro men, as also good ship-bread.

After Britain and France entered the war the fighting spread to Canada. There were only two feasible approaches to French Canada. One was by way of the St. Lawrence River, guarded at its mouth by Fort Louisburg on Cape Breton Island. An army of New Englanders, assisted by a British naval squadron, captured this outpost in 1745. However, the British made no effort to move on to Quebec, still 800 miles away, and attention shifted to the other avenue to Canada, the Lake Champlain waterway. A hundred-mile sliver of water wedged between the mountains of New York and those of Vermont, Lake Champlain was an ideal route for an invading army. Its southern arm, Lake George, lay only a few miles from New York's Hudson River. To the north the lake drained into the Richelieu River, which flowed into the St. Lawrence a few scant miles from Montreal, the fur-trading heart of French Canada.

An Anglo-American army assembled in Albany in the summer of 1746, and the call went to neighboring colonies for men and material. Maryland responded, as before, with several companies of soldiers, and Patrick Creagh stood ready with an assortment of services. In September the Assembly voted him 98 pounds, 7 shillings for maintaining thirty-two men at his house from July 8 to September 12. (Presumably, they tented in the backyard next to the kitchen, which was a separate structure.) It paid him another 11 pounds, 18 shillings, 9 pence for cleaning and repairing their arms. On August 10, Creagh's schooner *Hopewell* sailed from Annapolis with seventy-one men, and two days later his schooner *Hollister* embarked with eighty-four soldiers. Both vessels arrived in Albany on September 12. The Assembly paid Creagh £5 per man for the trip, plus 30 shillings per day for the use of one schooner and 40 shillings for the other. Creagh's return was slightly more than £1,000, and he received an additional £355 for another shipload of men in September. The attack on Canada never materialized, and there is no record of how the soldiers found their way back to Maryland.

Creagh's wartime profits were immediately invested in land. In 1746 he purchased a 500-acre farm at the head of the South River and another 120-acre tract along Dorsey Creek "outside the gate of the City of Annapolis." Within Annapolis he purchased three acres in the "Public Pasture," together with the buildings, wharfs, and the "commodities" therein. This probably was an expansion of his shipyard, land now occupied by the Naval Academy. He also purchased additional lots on Prince George Street.

Between 1749 and 1751, Creagh purchased additional tracts of county land — "Chance" on a branch of Curtis Creek, thirty-three acres near Beard's Creek, and eighty acres on Acton's Creek. An inventory of Creagh's estate made upon his death in 1760 indicates that he had an extensive hog and cattle operation on these lands, as well as wheat cultivation and flour mills. Creagh seems to have discovered the principle of "vertical integration," that is, controlling the entire process from farm to market: production, transportation, and retailing.

In the early 1750s Creagh also became a major player in the transatlantic tobacco trade. Notices frequently appeared in the *Maryland Gazette* that Creagh had available a full-rigged ship, often commanded by his son James, to carry tobacco to London on consignment. The trade was an arm of his shipbuilding business. In May 1754, for instance, he advertised a brand new vessel, the *Hanbury*, which had been built for the London firm of John Hanbury and Company. Creagh assured Maryland planters that the vessel would take an early departure because it was already a third full with a consignment to the Hanbury firm. Freight or passage could be obtained from Patrick Creagh in Annapolis, John Carnan in Baltimore Town, or James Creagh aboard the vessel.

Patrick's son James first appears in the historical record on October 18, 1748, when Dr. Charles Carroll and other members of the Baltimore Company paid him the sum of 58 pounds, 8 shillings "for goods bought of him for use of the Baltimore Ironworks." James had no doubt brought the goods from England, and the profit was quickly invested in land. In that same month he was recorded as the purchaser of 177 acres in Anne Arundel County. Three years later, when he made another purchase, he was described as a "mariner" residing in London. He was principally employed, it would seem, as captain of his father's tobacco ships. The voyage of May 1754 was his last; he disappeared thereafter from the historical record, either dead or banished by his father. James's last act in Maryland was to witness, on April 16, 1754, his father's signature on a contract that spelled ruin.

In the previous year, Patrick Creagh had somehow incurred a debt of £1,800 sterling to London merchants. Whether it was the result of a failed business venture on the part of James or an accident, such as a ship lost at sea, cannot be determined from the record. By the contract, recorded in September 1754, Creagh staked nearly everything he owned in Annapolis, including his own dwelling house, as security for the payment of the debt. He agreed to pay off the debt in annual installments of £360 sterling, with interest, and to sell the properties, if necessary, to meet the payments. The need to negotiate with his London creditors may have brought about his last trip across the Atlantic. On July 9, 1755, he advertised that he himself, as commander of the snow *Endeavor*, was prepared to load tobacco on consignment to London. Whether he actually made the voyage is not known.

What is known is that he utterly ignored the obligations of the indenture. He remained in his Annapolis dwelling and worked his county farms. Until his estate was finally settled, neither Creagh nor anyone else made a single payment on the debt.

Although Creagh's son James may have come to an unfortunate end, his daughter Elizabeth fared rather well. She married Richard Maccubbin, a prosperous merchant whose vessels had sailed along with Creagh's in the French war. When Creagh was forced to sell more lots in Annapolis in 1756 and 1757, Maccubbin was the purchaser. When Creagh died in 1760, leaving a tangled web of debt, Maccubbin sold enough of the county farmland to pay off the London indenture.

It was a sad ending for a life of such talent and ingenuity. Yet Creagh left his mark on Annapolis, and the city was much the better for it.

Aunt Lucy's Bake Shop

After Patrick Creagh's death, Thomas Rutland Sr., another Annapolis merchant, purchased the brick house on lot 95 from the London mortgagers for £350 sterling. Rutland apparently used it as a rental property. Sixteen years later, the Rutlands' grandson, Thomas Rutland Jr. obtained full title to the residence from Creagh's daughter, Elizabeth Maccubbin. The Maccubbins continued to prosper, as did their son, John Creagh Maccubbin, who purchased the house from Rutland in 1786. The price was £2,000, far in excess of its value, the sum apparently representing the payoff of a debt that Rutland owed Maccubbin. A tax assessor in 1798 valued the house at $150 and noted that it was in bad repair.

About that time John Smith, a free black, became a tenant of the property. He operated a carriage and carting business out of the house. On December 23, 1801, after the nation's capital had moved from Philadelphia to Washington, D. C., Smith placed an ad in the *Maryland Gazette* announcing the commencement of a stage line between Annapolis and Georgetown. The stages were to leave Annapolis every Thursday morning, pass through Bladensburg, and arrive at the Union

Tavern in Georgetown that evening. The return trip was made on Saturday. His livery stable was behind the house (later the site of a synagogue, and today the Chesapeake Bay Foundation). Smith's wife, "Aunt Lucy," operated a bake shop near the corner of Main and Green Streets, and the Creagh house ever after became known as "Aunt Lucy's Bake Shop." Smith was ultimately able to purchase the property, and it remained in the hands of his descendants until the Civil War.

Daniel Dulany, the Elder (1685–1753). Attributed to Justus Engelhardt Kuhn. *Courtesy of the Peabody Institute, on deposit at the Maryland Historical Society.*

3

Daniel Dulany:
From Servant to Gentleman

The predominant source of labor among the southern colonies in the seventeenth century was white indentured servants, initially from the British Isles, but increasingly, by the end of the century, from Germany. Lifetime slaves, brought from Africa or the Caribbean, did not replace the white servants until the beginning of the eighteenth century.

Short-term servitude (four to seven years) had long been known in Europe. Parents commonly placed their sons under bonded indenture to craftsmen so that they might learn trades. The indenture was carefully drawn to ensure that the lad actually received an education in return for his service. Persons who exchanged their labor for passage to America signed much simpler contracts. The terms of the indenture — typically negotiated between an emigrant and a ship captain — merely provided for passage to America and an agreement by the former to "truly serve his said master or his lawfull Assignees." The ship captain would then sell the indenture, upon arrival in America, to a planter or builder who needed labor. Only about half of the emigrants left England with formal indentures. The remainder merely agreed to serve according to the "custom of the country." A Maryland law of 1661 established customary service as four years for men and women who were twenty-two years or over at arrival. Younger persons were given terms of up to seven years, the length of term being decided by a county court.

Upon earning their freedom, usually in four to five years, the servants were allowed a certain amount of food and clothing. In Maryland the law required goods valued at £6 as a start in a free life (enough to buy a horse, a cow, and several pigs). The laws also sought to protect the most elementary rights of the servants, making it a crime to employ excessive brutality in punishment or risk of life. It was during the Atlantic crossing, in fact, where conditions were often the worst for the emigrants. A South Carolina planter pointed out that self-interest often prompted ship captains to take care of their cargoes of black slaves to preserve them for market, "but no other care was taken of those poor Protestant Christians from Ireland but to deliver as many as possible alive on Shoar upon the cheapest Terms." Since indentured servants only served four or five years, owners had little care for their health. Among those "poor Protestant Christians from Ireland" who landed on the Maryland shore was Daniel Dulany.

Those who spoke of "Protestant Christians from Ireland" usually referred to the transplanted Scots Presbyterians of northern Ireland. Dulany came from the Catholic South of Ireland, the bogs and meadows of Queen's County, where his ancestry could be traced back to the beginning of surnames in the late Middle Ages. He was born in 1685 in an impoverished countryside that had been ravished by the armies of Oliver Cromwell. Although his father had few resources, Dulany managed a certain amount of schooling and even entered the University of Dublin. While he was there, his father re-married, and Dulany felt that his chances of further support were limited. He left the university and joined his two brothers, who had decided to try their fortunes in America. They signed indentures to pay for the voyage. England and France went to war in 1703, the year they sailed, and their vessel joined a large convoy headed for the Chesapeake. Separating from the convoy after passing Cape Charles, the ship sailed up the Potomac River and anchored in Port Tobacco, seat of Charles County, Maryland.

Maryland was a natural choice for Irish immigrants. The Lords Baltimore had financed a skillful propaganda campaign among the

Irish in an effort to lure them to the Baltimores' Catholic refuge in America. Unfortunately, we know nothing of Dulany's religion before he landed in Maryland — whether he was raised a Protestant or experienced a shipboard conversion. We know only that he was a devoted Anglican throughout his life in Maryland. An indentured servant with a college education, even an incomplete one, was a rare species indeed, and Dulany was scooped up at dockside by George Plater, the most prominent attorney in southern Maryland. What arrangements his brothers made with local planters we do not know. Like the vast majority of white servants, they were absorbed into rural society and disappeared from the historical record.

George Plater had arrived in Maryland only fifteen years earlier. He, too, had the advantage of some education, and almost immediately he had begun the practice of law. Lawyers were few in Maryland, and because land transfers were complex, they were in high demand. Plater's practice grew rapidly, and it brought him to the attention of the governor. By the time he encountered Dulany, Plater held the offices of receiver of revenues for the Patuxent River district, naval officer of the Patuxent, and attorney general of the colony. By 1703 he had relinquished the post of attorney general because of the demands of his law practice. After the government was transferred from St. Mary's to Annapolis, Plater found attendance at court burdensome and time-consuming. He purchased Dulany's indenture in order to get help in drafting legal forms, tallying accounts, and copying letters. Because there were no law schools in America at the time, students learned the craft by serving an apprenticeship. Dulany thus became an apprentice in the law, just like any planter's son.

Dulany began immediately to lay the foundation for a professional career. The few books available were those of the great English jurists, like Sir Edward Coke. There was no record of Maryland law and no reports of decisions by Maryland courts. Dulany began a set of notebooks in which he recorded important cases and precedents set by court decisions. He maintained the notebooks all his life. He learned by example how to plead and prepare a brief. Unlike most apprentices in that planter society who sought an acquaintance with the law in order to better manage their business affairs, Dulany planned a career in the law. His indenture expired after four years, and about that same time Colonel Plater died. Dulany settled in Port Tobacco, and in August 1709 he was admitted to the bar of the Charles County Court.

Port Tobacco and Annapolis were the only villages on the western shore. The county courts that Dulany attended once a month otherwise consisted only of a courthouse and a tavern. Presiding over the courts were justices of the peace, most of them planters with only a meager acquaintance with the law. In addition to their judicial function, the judges were charged with a number of administrative duties: they appointed the overseers of roads and supervised their work; they licensed taverns, inns and, ferries and regulated their rates; they paid bounties for the killing of animals they regarded as pests such as crows and wolves; and they provided care for the indigent and orphans. In the courthouse were stored the records of births, marriages, and debts, as well as the all-important records of landholding.

Dulany performed well enough in his first year of practice, winning four of his first five cases. He caught the attention of the attorney general of the colony, who named him "Clerk of the Indictments and Prosecutor of her Majesty's Pleas" in Charles and St. Mary's counties. In 1710 Dulany was admitted to the bar in Prince George's County, an important step because Prince George's was the largest and wealthiest county in the province. The planters who resided on the rich bottom lands along the Potomac had the highest percentage of African slaves in the colony. For a lawyer who was soon to specialize in land transfers, Prince George's offered unlimited opportunity, for it extended into the unexplored interior as far as the Allegheny Ridge where the claims of Maryland's proprietors ran up against those of Virginia and Pennsylvania.

The practice of law proved quite lucrative. Each case in the county courts yielded a fee of 100 pounds of tobacco, worth about ten shillings sterling. This amounted to £100 sterling a year, a reasonably good living. In addition, Dulany could command much higher fees for arguing cases before the courts in Annapolis — the Provincial Court, the Chancery Court, and the High Court of Appeals. At the age of twenty-six he married the daughter of a local planter, Charity Courts, whose father had died leaving her a handsome dowry in land, slaves, cattle, and household effects. The marriage lasted only a year, for Charity died unexpectedly in late 1711. The dowry reverted to the Courts's estate, but Dulany was soon looking for other lands in which to invest his surplus income. In 1713 he moved to Nottingham Town in Prince George's County.

The war in Europe ended in that year, and the following year Queen Anne died. Her successor, a nondescript nobleman from Hanover in Germany, George I, brought to the throne a higher respect for contracts and charters than any of the Stuart sovereigns had evinced. He restored to the Lords Baltimore their Maryland proprietary. The Calvert family had retained title to the land, even during the period of royal rule, but they had difficulty in making land sales and in collecting quitrents (the rents owed to the proprietors by the planters who worked the land). The recovery of the right of governance gave the Calvert proprietors new opportunity to dispose of their uncharted and unsettled landholdings. The change would be of great importance to the career of Daniel Dulany.

In June 1713 Dulany purchased a plantation near Nottingham, 178 acres of arable land with a dwelling and storehouses, for the sum of £50 sterling and 2,000 pounds of tobacco. Later that summer he purchased two additional tracts across the Patuxent River in Calvert County. A landed estate brought social status. Court records had previously referred to him as "Mr. Dulany." He now became "Daniell Dullany of Prince George's County, gentleman." To rise from servant to gentleman in the space of ten years would have been unheard of in England or Ireland. Nor was it common even in America's relatively fluid society. Dulany managed it through a combination of skill and good fortune.

In the course of his practice before the Calvert County Court Dulany no doubt made the acquaintance of Colonel Walter Smith, justice of the peace, colonel of militia, and representative of Calvert County in the lower house of the Assembly. Smith's lineage dated back to the earliest settlers in the county, and he had extensive lands. He died in 1711 leaving a widow and eight children. The youngest of Smith's daughters, Rebecca, turned seventeen in the year that Dulany first appeared in the records as "gentleman." They were married shortly thereafter, and he brought Rebecca to Nottingham.

Dulany's practice continued to expand both in the county courts and in Annapolis. By 1715 it was not uncommon for him to have fifty or sixty cases on the docket of the Provincial Court in a single session. Each case tried in Annapolis yielded a fee of £2 sterling, a sum that was prescribed by law. Possession of such ready cash was a tremendous advantage in a society where currency was so scarce that most transactions were made in tobacco. He systematically added to his landholdings in Prince George's by snatching bargains as they came on the market. He hired an overseer to manage his plantations, and by 1719 he had acquired nineteen African slaves. When his holdings became too extensive for his overseer to manage, he leased lands to persons who aspired to become planters. In that way his lands yielded an annual return while their value rose over time. By 1720, with a total acreage of 27,200, he was one of the largest landholders in the colony. To this point he had carefully avoided politics, but his wealth and public spirit made entry into the political scene all but inevitable.

Through the seventeenth century the Lords Baltimore, imitating the Stuart monarchs, ruled Maryland as a personal fiefdom. They appointed governors, summoned and discharged assemblies, and dispensed justice. Their only obligation to the crown was the payment of two Indian arrows a year at Easter time. (Maryland was held as a fief from the king; this was the "rent.") For most of the century the elected Assembly was a rubber stamp for the proprietor's edicts. It did not even have the power to levy taxes and appropriate funds (the "power of the purse") for its first half-century of existence. During the period of royal rule after 1690 the Assembly matured rapidly. Under Governor Nicholson it boldly asserted that Marylanders had all the rights and privileges of Englishmen. It gained new confidence during Maryland's last years as a royal colony, from 1709 to 1714, when the distracted government of Queen Anne neglected to name a governor and left the colony to run itself. Marylanders during the years of royal rule were also absorbing the doctrines of English Whiggery, the centerpiece of which was the concept of legislative supremacy. In England, by the early eighteenth century, the crown had virtually abandoned any pretense that it had the power to veto an act of Parliament. In Maryland a dispute between governor and Assembly over the proprietor's right to disallow laws was the opening shot in a half-century of political warfare that culminated in revolution.

After their province was restored to them in 1715 the Baltimore proprietors were content to leave in charge John Hart, the last royal governor. Hart, however, was continually at odds with the newly energized Assembly, and he carried on bitter feuds with Maryland officials. In an effort to end the bickering, the fifth Lord Baltimore sent to Maryland a member of his own family, Charles Calvert, to serve as governor. Calvert landed in the summer of 1720 and convened his first Assembly on October 12.

By 1720, the Assembly of Maryland, like those of the other colonies, had developed rules and procedures that consciously imitated those of the British House of Commons. At the opening of each new Assembly the lower house would choose a speaker, who would be presented to the governor in the same way that the speaker of the House of Commons was presented to the king. The speaker would then petition the governor for recognition of the fundamental privileges of the house. These included freedom from arrest during the session, freedom of speech on the floor of the house, and a promise that a favorable construction would be put on the proceedings of the house. After the governor ratified these privileges, the body proceeded to nominate standing committees and establish rules for its own self-government. The rules all came from English tradition: no member could be called by name on the floor, tardiness was prohibited, firearms were forbidden, and fines were set for violations.

In his opening address to the Assembly Governor Calvert revealed his utter ignorance of the colony's institutional development. He spoke to Marylanders in the language of the seventeenth century, assuring the gentlemen of the upper and lower houses of the Lord Proprietor's "Benign sweet disposition," and he showed them Baltimore's own command to bring "our Prerogative" and "your Privileges . . . into Balance." Calvert was certain that Lord Baltimore's aim was to treat "the good People of Maryland as a Bountiful Indulgent Father towards a dutiful Deserving son." The governor then disclosed what was meant by "our Prerogative" when he revealed that his Lordship had disallowed two acts passed by the previous Assembly. The intellectual chasm between governor and Assembly widened in the next few years. Calvert talked of "Prerogative," "Privilege," and Lord Baltimore's "Instructions." The Assembly spoke, not of privilege, but of "our happy Constitution," by which it sought to elevate to the realm of higher law the body of precedent accumulated in the previous quarter-century.

Daniel Dulany was drawn into the fray after he moved to Annapolis in the autumn of 1720. The move was necessitated by his growing practice in the provincial courts. He was spending more and more time in Annapolis and the journey from Nottingham, whether by coastal schooner or horseback, was time-consuming and troublesome. He was not a planter at heart, and the overseer of his Prince George's plantations was a man of ability and integrity — rare qualities in men of that occupation. That allowed Dulany to leave the countryside for the city.

Although it had been designated a "City" by the Assembly, Annapolis in 1720 was still a struggling community of forty houses, most of them wooden. The shallowness of its harbor had retarded commercial development, but the Assembly had made a generous effort to attract artisans and retail merchants by offering free lots on Powder Hill (where St. John's College is today). Grouped around the statehouse circle were the houses of government officials, planters who were only part-time residents of Annapolis but who provided some cultural quality and social interchange. Governor Calvert's marriage to a daughter of a local planter and the accompanying festivities boosted the city's reputation as the social center of the colony.

Dulany's first step on the road to political preferment came in the spring of 1721 when the parishioners of St. Anne's Church elected him to the vestry. In Maryland, as well as Virginia, the Anglican vestry was composed of the more important men of the community, and it had a number of social responsibilities beyond its administrative duty of selecting and paying the parish priest. It provided relief to the poor, found homes for orphans, and kept track of the conduct of church members. Its functions were supported by a tax on the community, payable in tobacco. When tobacco prices fell, the vestry suffered, as did the pay of its minister. Dulany, who took his duties as vestryman seriously, kept St. Anne's solvent through the hard times of the 1720s by purchasing the donated tobacco at London prices, thereby absorbing personally the cost of shipping and marketing.

Later in 1721, Dulany was elected to the city council of Annapolis, and in 1722 the voters sent him to the lower house of the Assembly. There Dulany allied himself with Thomas Bordley, an Annapolis attorney who was the emerging leader of the Country Party. Named to the committee of laws, the pair brought the strife between governor and Assembly into focus with a resolution on the courts of justice. The resolution proposed to insert into the oath taken by all judges a clause that would oblige them to render decisions "According to the Laws Statutes Ordinances and reasonable Customs of England and of this Province." Further, the judges were to treat all inhabitants of Maryland equally without regard to any instructions to the contrary from the king or the proprietor. The clear purpose of the Bordley-Dulany resolution was to absorb into Maryland law the great body of English statute and common law, from the Magna Carta to the Bill of Rights of 1691. This was law that the proprietor could not disallow, and the resolution would prevent him from interfering with the judges' application of it. It amounted to nothing less than a constitutional revolution. The upper house of the Assembly (men appointed by the proprietor who also functioned as the Governor's Council) recognized the implications of the lower house's resolution, and they postponed it to the following session.

Dulany lost his seat in the Assembly in 1725 (many Annapolis voters were officeholders subject to influence by the governor), and he resumed his law practice. Bordley nevertheless managed to keep the subject of constitutional reform before the legislature and hence the public. Dulany, meanwhile, immersed himself in the Whig writings of the previous century. He was particularly intrigued by the developing philosophy of natural law. This was a weapon of longer intellectual reach than the reliance on English legal precedent. It allowed a colonial theorist to argue that certain rights, such as liberty and property, were endowed upon mankind by a higher law, and they could not be abridged by any temporal ruler.

In the autumn of 1728, Dulany published a thirty-one page pamphlet under the title *The Rights of the Inhabitants of Maryland* to the Benefit of the English Laws. The issue, he explained to his readers, was

> whether a People are to be governed by Laws, which their Mother Country has experimentally found, to be beneficial to Society. . . . Or whether, They are to be governed by the Discretion (as some People softly term the *Caprice*, and *Arbitrary Pleasure*) of any Set of Men.

He quoted from the cardinal documents of English constitutional history from Magna Carta to the Petition of Right. Although he contended that the colonists had all the rights and liberties of British subjects, he did not want to bind Maryland to the laws of England alone. He borrowed from John Locke's *Second Treatise* the concept of the natural rights of free individuals that antedated government, and he endorsed Locke's conception of a social contract by which government was created. Dulany's pamphlet stands as the first important statement of the American view of the imperial relationship. Marylanders quoted from it for decades to come, long after he himself had abandoned its radical principles.

Daniel Dulany was forty-five years old in 1730. His portrait reveals a man full in the flesh, without being overweight. His eyes look squarely at the viewer from a full ruddy face. If he had ever suffered illness, the record does not reveal it. For two decades he had maintained a heavy schedule of court appearances with scarcely a missed

No drawing of Daniel Dulany's house on Church Circle has survived. This house was built by Daniel Jr. and photographed in 1805. *Maryland Historical Society.*

date or a tardy brief. The Dulanys' eldest son, Daniel Jr, had been born in 1722; the couple had two more sons and three daughters by the early 1730s. The parents prescribed the destinies of all six children. Dulany decided that his eldest son would follow his own career in law and politics; Daniel Jr. was sent to England for schooling at Eton and then Cambridge. His second son, Walter, seemed to have a practical turn of mind, so he was apprenticed to a Philadelphia merchant. Dulany planned to put him in charge of his own mercantile investments. The youngest son, Dennis, went to sea, as younger sons often did in those days. The three daughters, Rebecca, Rachel, and Margaret, were all destined to become the wives of tobacco planters. At the moment, however, they, together with the three daughters of

Councilor Benjamin Tasker, were content to enliven the Annapolis social scene.

In the 1720s Dulany had turned his investment strategy to the unclaimed proprietary lands of the upper Potomac valley. The procedure for obtaining vacant land was quite complicated; hence a lawyer had a decided advantage. A person desiring land went to the proprietor's land office in Annapolis. After he made a down payment, the judge of the land office issued a warrant authorizing the purchase of a certain amount of land. The warrant went to the surveyor general, who passed it on to the deputy surveyor of the county in which the desired tract lay. The deputy surveyed the land and returned to the examiner general a certificate describing the location of the tract and its boundaries. There was no requirement that the survey be rectangular or that it abut other holdings. Consequently, only the most fertile land came under survey, and rocky, sandy or swampy land in between, of assorted shapes and sizes, remained in the hands of the proprietor.

When Dulany began speculating in western lands, he realized that he needed a partner, a man on the spot who could arrange for the survey of only the best lands. His choice was Major John Bradford, a Prince George's planter with an intimate knowledge of the Monocacy River valley and the lands beyond the Catoctin hills. Bradford was also a surveyor. Dulany dealt with Annapolis officialdom, aided by his ability to pay cash for warrants; Bradford surveyed thousands of acres of bottom land along the Potomac. When the surveys were completed, Dulany advertised for tenants; Bradford showed the land and arranged terms of tenure. Quitrents owed to the proprietor might have cut into their profits, but the Assembly and the proprietor had reached an agreement on that problem in 1717. The Assembly levied a tax of two shillings per hogshead on all exported tobacco, and this was conveyed to the proprietor in lieu of rents. Although the yield from the tax was somewhat less than the theoretical value of the quit rents, the proprietor was agreeable because it eliminated bookkeeping costs and other overhead. As a result of his partnership with Bradford, Dulany became the largest landholder in western Maryland.

The proprietor himself, Charles Calvert, Fifth Baron Baltimore, sailed to Maryland in the fall of 1732. Dulany left no record of his relations with the proprietor during the six months that Lord Baltimore personally governed the colony, but somehow the two men took the measure of one another. A bargain was struck that altered the direction of Dulany's life.

Why Dulany shifted sides and became the leading defender of proprietary power and interest can only be surmised. In the late 1720s he had been given a taste of what the Whig doctrine of legislative supremacy might yield in practice. The Assembly, dominated by planters of modest means, passed a law that drastically lowered the fees that lawyers could charge for handling court cases. The law was passed despite the opposition of the two Country Party leaders, Dulany and Phillip Hammond, and both men ceased the practice of law. The fee law was disallowed by the proprietor, and the two resumed their practices. The incident was a valuable lesson for Dulany in the potential excesses of democracy and the value of executive restraints.

Money was another incentive for Dulany's conversion. The proprietor rained offices upon him, and Dulany ended up with two of the most lucrative in the province. Astonishingly, all this was accomplished without much criticism, either in Annapolis society or in the halls of the Assembly. Loyalty to principle was not a cardinal virtue in Maryland society, and the élite never allowed political differences to intrude on their social and commercial activities. Dr. Charles Carroll, who became the new leader of the Country Party in the lower house, remained a partner of Dulany in an ironworks in Baltimore County for decades thereafter.

Lord Baltimore had come to Maryland to put his own revenues in order. He allied himself with Dulany simply to ensure that he had a competent watchdog for his interests after he returned to England. When the Assembly met in March 1733, Baltimore revealed the new order. Instead of proposing laws and regulations for Assembly action, he issued a series of edicts. His central concern was quitrents. The compromise of 1717 had not been a permanent settlement; it had to be renewed every three years. And each time the Assembly had used the occasion to extract concessions from the governor. Baltimore wanted a permanent system, and he chose to return to the collection of quitrents, even though it meant organizing a collection service. A second edict directed that the governor's salary be paid out of the tax on exported tobacco. This deprived the Assembly of any leverage over the governor. Baltimore's final concern was the pay of colonial officials. This too he resolved by proclamation, establishing a table of fees for the support of proprietary officers. By accomplishing all this without asking for or receiving any input from the Assembly, Baltimore was reasserting the dominance of the executive in the Maryland government. The Country Party could only stand helplessly and watch.

To ensure the permanence of his new arrangement, Lord Baltimore conferred on Dulany the offices of agent, attorney general, and judge of the Court of Vice Admiralty. Of these the most lucrative was the office of chief agent and receiver general, for he received a salary of £100 sterling plus a percentage of the rents collected. The position also entailed a special relationship with the land office, a boon to any land speculator. A year later Dulany exchanged offices with Councilor Tasker and became commissary general, an office equally rewarding and with more power. Whenever the governor died (as Charles Calvert did in that year) or left the province, Dulany was the chief executive of the colony.

Lord Baltimore's "revolution of 1733" had no lasting impact on the evolution of Maryland's "happy constitution." The Country Party revived by the end of the decade under the skillful leadership of Dr. Charles Carroll, and in the war years of the 1740s it found new ways to exercise leverage against the governor. Dulany remained in the lower house to lead the Court Party, a role that earned him annual reelection by the voters of Annapolis. When he finally tired of being in a perpetual minority, he made it known that he would accept an appointment to the governor's Council. Baltimore issued the appropriate instruction to Governor Thomas Bladen who arrived in the colony in 1742. Dulany quit his seat in the lower house and was sworn in as a member of his Lordship's Council of State on September 25, 1742.

In the mid-1730s, Rebecca gave birth to a seventh child, another daughter, and then her health failed. She died in March 1737 at the age of forty-one. A year and a half later Dulany married for the third time. His bride was the widow Henrietta Maria Chew, whose husband had died at the age of thirty-two, leaving her with six children under the age of ten. They were similar in age to Dulany's youngest, which no doubt made for a raucous household. Dulany's house had ample room for the new company. It was a sturdy mansion, probably of brick, to the south of the church circle (the site of the county court-house today) with lawn and garden extending uphill to the circle. Through her connections with both the Lloyd and the Chew families, Henrietta Maria also brought under Dulany's management tobacco plantations on both shores of the bay.

That same year, 1737, Daniel Jr. completed his studies in Latin and Greek at Eton and entered Clare College, Cambridge. In 1742 he entered the Middle Temple at the Inns of Court, London. Upon his departure in 1747 he was called to the Bar, an honor accorded to only a few and almost never to an American.

Dulany's lands in western Maryland were rapidly becoming popu-lated in the 1740s. Scots-Irish and German immigrants, who had land-ed in Philadelphia and followed the wagon road to the west were channeled by the mountains into the Monocacy and Antietam valleys of Maryland, and on to the Shenandoah valley of Virginia. The increase in population soon raised the question of the exact boundary between Maryland and Virginia. Virginia, based on its "sea to sea" grant of 1609, claimed the entire west, including the "island of California." Maryland's western boundary had been defined by its charter as "the first Fountain of the River Pottowmack." The question was which remote rivulet in the mountains constituted the "first Fountain." Dulany investigated and made the exciting discovery (which he instantly communicated to Lord Baltimore) that west of the Shenandoah the Potomac divided into two large branches, "one called the South and the other the North branch." The South Branch, Dulany was informed, was the larger of the two, and if the proprietor could make good a claim to that he would possess what is today the eastern third of West Virginia.

Dulany apparently was given this information by his new partner in the western venture, Thomas Cresap, a burly Irishman who had originally settled on the disputed Maryland-Pennsylvania boundary near the mouth of the Susquehanna River. Insisting that his farm was in Maryland, he conducted a one-man war against the colony of Pennsylvania. After mauling two posses that were sent to arrest him, he was finally overpowered and put in jail in Philadelphia. Dulany obtained his freedom and lent him money to buy a farm in the west. In return, Cresap surveyed Dulany's warrants into small parcels and sold them to German migrants.

After learning of the two branches of the Potomac, Dulany himself made a reconnaissance of the area. He started too late in the year and never made it as far as the South Branch. What he did see, however, was the astonishing fertility of the valleys of western Maryland, where eons of erosion had produced a loam topsoil that measured three feet in some places. Given the fertility of the land and the flow of pioneers, Dulany could see a fortune to be made in empire-building. Upon his return to Annapolis in late 1744 he devoted nearly all of his energies to the western venture.

Dulany's previous purchases had been along river courses, the Patuxent and the Potomac. Rivers were essential for a successful plantation, for tobacco, packed into 100-pound hogsheads, was too heavy to be transported long distances by land. The character of the western population gave Dulany a new inspiration. He began taking out warrants on tracts in the Monacacy valley remote from the river, which itself seemed a dubious commercial route to Cheasapeake Bay-bound planters. His Annapolis neighbors were amazed by his new acquisitions and predicted his ultimate bankruptcy. The method in his madness was the realization that German people moving into the area had no knowledge of, or interest in, tobacco culture. They were cereal farmers, and they could survive indefinitely on a crop of wheat or rye, with a few farm animals, until cities and flour mills sprouted in the west.

Annapolis connections paid off as always. Dulany's friend Benjamin Tasker had patented many years earlier 7,000 acres along the Monocacy River. It was called "Tasker's Chance." Although it had never been subdivided or improved, German squatters were working the land. After reaching an oral agreement with the squatters, Dulany purchased the property for £2,000 Maryland money. For a price of five shillings, eight pence an acre, he came into possession of an oblong tract extending five miles along the Monocacy River and stretching west to the Catoctin mountains. With the help of Cresap, Dulany divided the tract into farm units of 100 to 300 acres each and sold them to the German squatters at prices below cost. He kept the price low in part because of his appreciation for German farmers as ideal pioneers. Their industry and thrift would improve land prices everywhere.

But he also had in mind a town and future city. Near the eastern boundary of "Tasker's Chance" a creek that wound down from the Catoctins to the Monocacy provided a nice backdrop for a town site. In the autumn of 1745 Dulany and his surveyor laid out a grid of intersecting streets and measured 340 lots, each with a street frontage of sixty feet. He christened the future city Frederick Town, a name which, according to convenience, could be interpreted as an honor to the son and heir of Lord Baltimore, or the Crown Prince of Great Britain, or the King of Prussia. He urged both the Reformed and the Lutheran churches to erect buildings in the town, and he donated lots to both. Not surprisingly, most of the Frederick Town lots were taken up by craftsmen with German names, who maintained houses and shops under the same roof. Delighted with this accretion of population in his province, Lord Baltimore issued Dulany a patent authorizing weekly markets in the town "for buying and Selling all sorts of Cattle and other provisions of every kind," as well as the right to hold two annual fairs, in May and October.

Dulany's second son, Walter, had completed his apprenticeship in Philadelphia and was put to work on his father's commercial and money-lending businesses. In December 1745 the Annapolis electorate sent him to the lower house of the Assembly where he made himself into a workhorse for the proprietary interest. After returning from England, Daniel Jr. married one of Benjamin Tasker's daughters, and his father cast about for an Assembly seat that would launch him on a political career. Newborn Frederick Town was a clear possibility. The residents of the Monocacy Valley were already complaining about the expense of time and energy required to attend Prince George's County Court. With help from Walter, Dulany induced the Assembly to create a new county. Prince George's retained approximately its present boundaries, and the rest of western Maryland was elevated to Frederick County, with the county seat at Frederick Town.

The new county was organized just in time to choose its first delegates in the general election called for March 1749. Dulany himself journeyed to Frederick Town to work on behalf of his son. The effort seemed to pay off, as Daniel Jr. managed to edge in as the fourth member of the county delegation. Unfortunately, when the Assembly convened it was met by two petitions from the county alleging fraud in the returns. This was prime fare for Dulany's foes in the Country Party, and Daniel Jr. lost his seat. After a debate behind closed doors, the house passed a resolution denouncing "uncommon Entertainments and great Quantities of strong and spiritous liquors" at elections. It seems that father may have overdone it. In the following election the Dulanys worked the limited electorate (Germans, unaccustomed to elections, normally did not vote at this time) with more finesse, and Daniel Jr. won a seat. He remained a force in Maryland politics until the Revolution, seeking desperately to reconcile imperial interests with colonial rights. In the end, when the Revolution broke out, he declared himself a neutral.

Realizing that no man is immortal, Dulany began dividing his property between his surviving sons in 1748. He may well have consulted their preferences, but in the end the distribution was in accord with his own designs for their futures. To Walter he deeded two warehouses in Annapolis together with the adjacent waterfront. He also gave him vacant tracts of land, totaling 6,000 acres, in Baltimore County. To his eldest son he entrusted the development of the empire he had amassed in the west. To both of his sons, jointly, he gave his interest in the Baltimore Iron Works, by then perhaps the most valuable of his assets.

Because Dulany and his Carroll family partners had systematically reinvested the proceeds, the business had new furnaces, a forge, 20,000 acres of timberland as a source of charcoal, a labor force of slaves and indentured servants, and a sloop for delivering the product to markets in England. The third son, Dennis, does not appear in the bequests and may have been lost at sea.

The Frederick County election of 1751, in which Daniel Jr. had won his seat in the Assembly, was Dulany's last effort in politics. Thereafter he retired to his Annapolis study with the books he had collected and a heavy correspondence. Governor Ogle, with whom he had worked through the late 1740s, died suddenly in the fall of 1751, and Dulany's health began to fail about the same time. Dr. Charles Carroll visited him in the fall of 1752 and informed his son (Charles Carroll "the Barrister") that the councilor could not last much longer. "By the Appearance of his Countenance," Carroll wrote, "I should Judge that by Next May Sun would scarce warm him." Dulany in fact lasted into the following summer, although he was unable to attend Council meetings after November. In the late summer of 1753 he wrote out directions for the disposal of the autumn harvest of his plantations. It was his final act before his stalwart constitution succumbed to mortality.

4

Dr. Charles Carroll:
The Physician as Merchant

Maryland in 1715 — the year in which Dr. Charles Carroll is thought to have landed on its shores — was still encumbered with a reputation for being a land of death. The Chesapeake colonies, Maryland and Virginia, had been zones of pestilence since their founding. The birthrate did not exceed the rate of death until about 1700; through the seventeenth century immigration was the only source of population increase. And adaptation to the American environment — a process known as "seasoning" — took a heavy toll. One colonist was of the opinion that one out of three immigrants died within a year after arriving in the colony. Even those who survived this conditioning could not expect to live long. Half of those who landed in Maryland in their early twenties (the average age of an immigrant) would be dead by the age of forty; 70 per cent would be dead before the age of fifty.

Malaria, probably imported from Africa in the blood cells of slaves, and typhoid, caused by contaminated water, were endemic throughout the Chesapeake. Scurvy was prevalent in the wintertime, especially among the poor, who lived on a diet of meat and cereal. Bathing was rare generally and particularly among the poor and the unlettered, and body lice was a common affliction. The lice carried the typhus microbe, causing a sickness commonly known as "jail fever" (because jail rats also carried lice). Those who managed to survive these maladies were left in such weak condition that they often succumbed to pulmonary infections or the dreaded small pox.

Trained physicians were scarce everywhere in British America. Of the 3,500 doctors practicing on the eve of the Revolution only 10 per cent had any formal medical training and only half of those had medical degrees. While some Americans went to Britain for medical training, Englishmen with medical degrees — "Doctors of Physick" — simply did not come to America. Physicians in Britain were members of a select guild with high social status. Like other members of the upper class, they had no motive to uproot themselves and move to the New World. Surgeons were a lesser breed. They were not permitted the title of doctor; they were addressed simply as mister. Originally lumped in the same guild with barbers, surgeons received no formal training and did not obtain their own company until 1745. They learned their craft on the job, usually in the army or navy. The first "doctors" in Maryland were naval surgeons, who settled in the colony after tiring of the sea.

Pharmacy was a third specialty with its own guild. Apothecaries were originally members of the grocers' guild, but in 1617 they obtained an organization of their own. Thereafter grocers were forbidden to sell drugs. Apothecaries had a certain amount of social status because they were the source of the vegetable and mineral remedies prescribed by physicians. Medical thought in 1700 had identified only a few specific diseases: consumption (tuberculosis), smallpox, and the Great Pox (syphilis). Other illnesses were simply viewed as stemming from a morbid condition of the body humors, which produced certain symptoms — chills, fever, vomiting, or diarrhea. The medicines prescribed by physicians were aimed at symptomatic relief.

In America, where guilds did not exist and social classes were fluid, the three branches of British medicine merged into one. There were no medical schools until a medical faculty was added to the College of Philadelphia in 1765 and no professional examining board or licensing restrictions until New Jersey created a board in 1772. As a result, Americans called anyone with medical skills a doctor. Significantly, Charles Carroll, who apparently had some medical training but almost certainly did not have a medical degree, began referring to himself as Dr. Carroll as soon as he stepped off the boat.

The Carrolls of Ireland could trace their lineage back to the beginnings of Irish surnames in the eleventh century. Over the centuries they had intermarried with Irish royalty and acquired extensive lands, estimated by one writer to have been upwards of 379,000 acres in Tipperary and neighboring counties. Most of this wealth vanished upon the English conquest of Ireland in the seventeenth century. In the 1650s, Cromwell's army swept across Ireland, confiscating the estates of all who resisted and turning the lands over to a new English ruling class. Irish Catholics won a brief respite under the later Stuarts, Charles II and his Catholic brother James II, but then James was swept from the throne in the Revolution of 1688. James landed in Ireland the following year with a shipload of French gold and arms. He recruited an army, lost a battle to King William, and fled back to France, leaving the Irish to ruin themselves in his cause.

William completed the confiscation of Irish estates, and the English Parliament passed penal laws limiting the amount of land that Catholics could own and barring them from trades, professions, public office, and the electoral process. Those who could afford to do so emigrated to France or America. Dr. Charles Carroll moved to Maryland with his wife Mary Blake, daughter of a prominent family of Hampshire, England. His only brother John was lost at sea while attempting to emigrate to the British West Indies. Late in Carroll's life, a cousin, Sir Daniel O'Carroll of London, offered to help Charles recover some of the castles and lands to which he was sole heir, but Carroll declined, feeling that it was hopeless to engage in a legal battle with the English landlords who controlled the political and judicial system.

Ironically, Catholicism was not one of the impediments that he faced. He had been raised a Roman Catholic, as were all members of the Carroll family, but he landed in Maryland a confirmed Protestant. It seems likely that he converted to the Church of England upon his marriage. However, he was also aware that Maryland, especially after the removal of the capital to Annapolis, was governed by loyal

Anglicans. For a man who all his life kept his eye on the main chance, a shipboard conversion would have been in character.

The obituary that appeared in the *Maryland Gazette* upon Dr. Carroll's death in 1755 stated that he had arrived in Maryland in 1715. A somewhat earlier date seems likely because an account book that he began in the following year reveals a medical practice that extended into nearly every county in the colony. His fee was 100 pounds of tobacco, or a multiple of that for some extraordinary service. The medicines he prescribed evidently were included in the fee. He also seems to have functioned as a pharmacist, selling drugs on a retail basis. The account book indicates that he purchased his medicines from an agent in London. The nature and variety of his purchases provide an interesting insight into eighteenth-century medicine.

The orders were made annually, and nearly all included a request for rhubarb. A nineteenth-century *Materia Medica* (manual for pharmacists) explains that the rhubarb used for medicinal purposes was obtained from the root of a plant that "resembles the pie plant" and was grown in Asia. The active ingredients were organic acids, and it was administered as a stomach-settling tonic. Calomel was another standard item on the doctor's order form. This was a chloride of mercury, made by combining mercury with table salt. It was widely used in surgery because, like all mercury compounds, it was an antiseptic. Carroll and his fellow practitioners had no concept of germs or viruses as an explanation of disease, but they were observant clinicians content to use anything that worked. Calomel also killed body lice and cured skin diseases like ringworm.

Other standard features of Dr. Carroll's medicine chest were opium, used as a sedative and pain reliever, and sal ammoniac. This was a white powder, ammonium chloride, that could be dissolved in water. It was administered as an expectorant for lung diseases, such as pneumonia or tuberculosis. It was also considered an analgesic that relieved the pain of sprains, bruises, and rheumatism.

Dr. Carroll also purchased large quantities of barley. One order specified twelve pounds of "pearl" and twelve pounds of "French" barley. Fermented into a malt, these ingredients produced diastase, peptise, and sugar, making an all-purpose stomach tonic particularly useful for convalescents who were having trouble digesting starches. Licorice was another medicine ordered in large quantities. It was administered as a demulcent that soothed inflamed membranes of the nose or throat and was also used to flavor some of the bitter-tasting medicines. Rounding out the doctor's order form were "English saffron," which helped relieve gout by stimulating the release of uric acid, and jalap, a harsh-acting body purge, prescribed for constipation and edema ("dropsy").

Dr. Carroll apparently found his retail business more lucrative and less time-consuming, for he soon abandoned his medical practice. Fees paid for medical services in tobacco certificates disappear from his account book by 1719. He continued to import medicines, but he also began importing clothing and tools, such as hoes, axes, and shovels. An order of 1725 included 100 yards of "welsh cotton," four dozen pairs of men's "yarn hose, coarse" and 100 ells (an English measure equal to 45 inches) of white "oznabrigg" (a coarse, loosely woven cotton). The following year he sent four hogsheads of tobacco to London and ordered fifty-six pounds of "glew," twelve barrels of lamp black, twenty gallons of linseed oil, and twenty "tables" of "Crown glass" cut into "Ranges 7 inches high." That same year he entered the West Indies trade, sending a hundredweight of beeswax (used for candles) to a merchant in Barbados, with a request that "you will dispose to best advantage." The retail business was clearly profitable. By the mid-1720s, Carroll had a vessel of his own, and his annual export of tobacco had risen from four or five hogsheads to fifty.

He had also begun to acquire land. As early as 1718 he obtained his first tract of 2,400 acres from Charles Carroll, a distant relative and the head of the proprietor's land office. (Known as "The Settler," this Carroll was the father of Charles Carroll of Annapolis and grandfather of Charles Carroll of Carrollton.) Before the lands of western Maryland became available, Dr. Carroll specialized in lands that had escheated to the proprietor when a planter died without heirs. The proprietor's agents were happy to convey the property so they could collect quitrents on it. After Frederick County was formed, Dr. Carroll became as active as Daniel Dulany in speculating in western land warrants. He eventually held patents to ninety-six tracts totaling 31,529 acres, for an average of 352 acres per holding. Of these he sold fifty-seven tracts containing 22,781 acres, at a profit margin that frequently reached 400 per cent. The proceeds, however, were slow in arriving because of the chronic shortage of money in Maryland, and the merchant-speculator was often strapped for cash.

The doctor's family increased along with his wealth. In March 1723, Mary gave birth to a son who was given the name of his father. (To the utter confusion of posterity, this would be the fourth of five Charles Carrolls to reside in Annapolis.) In 1727, the couple had a daughter, whom they named Mary Clare. She would eventually marry Nicholas Maccubbin, a wealthy Annapolis merchant and first cousin to Patrick Creagh's son-in-law, Richard Maccubbin. A third offspring, John Henry Carroll, whom the doctor affectionately called "Jacky," entered the world in 1731. This growing family was comfortably housed in a large brick and wood-frame house located on the corner of Church Street (now Main Street) and Conduit Street. The L-shaped structure probably also accommodated the doctor's pharmacy and dry goods store.

By the end of the 1720s Dr. Carroll's retail establishment was beginning to take on the appearance of a modern chain store in terms of the variety and quantity of goods offered. An order placed with a London merchant included two barrels of gunpowder, two hundredweight of "Swan and Duck Shot," twenty pounds of colored thread, four dozen "Men's felt Hatts," a dozen "Grubbing Axes," six "Ruggs of about 12/6," and 200 ells "best Hempen ropes." The list incidentally revealed just how dependent Maryland was on the mother country for manufactured articles.

Acutely aware of Maryland's need to diversify, Dr. Carroll entered into a partnership in 1731 to build an ironworks. His partners were Daniel Dulany, Benjamin Tasker, wealthiest of the Annapolis merchants, Charles Carroll of Annapolis (son of The Settler) and the latter's brother, Daniel Carroll. Daniel, the only member of the firm who was not a resident of Annapolis, had extensive tobacco lands in Prince George's County. The partnership, which named itself The Baltimore Company, planned to mine iron ore on a 1,300-acre tract that Dr. Carroll had purchased on the north bank of the Patapsco River. The potential for an iron industry in Maryland had already been demonstrated by the Principio Company (formed by English ironmasters in 1718), which had a furnace in Cecil County at the head of Chesapeake Bay. Within a decade this company had become one of the largest producers of iron in British America.

Since the Baltimore partnership knew nothing of ironmaking, Dr. Carroll directed a series of questions to an ironmaster of Philadelphia concerning the construction of the furnace, the cost of "raising" a ton of ore, the wages of laborers, and the cost of refining a ton of pig iron into bar iron. Pig iron, the initial result of the burning of ore with charcoal, contained too much carbon to be usable, and it had to be fired a second time in a forge before it could be "wrought" into tools.

The Philadelphian's reply was quick and detailed. Cost and profitability, he insisted, were a matter of good management. A good manager, he advised, attended to detail and was constantly on guard against "Pretenders." His own furnace was thirty feet square, of the same height, and built of stone. With respect to production, he said, the general rule was that two and one half to three tons of ore yielded a ton of pig iron. The amount of charcoal required to make a ton of iron was about two and one-half loads, each load containing 120 bushels. Two and one half cords of wood were needed to make one load of coal. Each furnace was controlled by a founder, a skilled workman who regulated the heat and built the casting bed, consisting of a main feeder and side molds for cooling the molten iron. (The casting bed resembled, to a person with some imagination, a sow and her suckling piglets; hence the name "pig iron.") A furnace could be kept going with a crew of five: two to dig the ore and three to break it up and burn it. Using the figures given him, Dr. Carroll calculated that the construction of a furnace and related buildings, the purchase of twenty-six black slaves at £30 each, wages for skilled workers, and shipping costs would total £5,615 sterling. That was about equal to the price in England of 500 tons of pig iron, which he figured the furnace could produce (and hence pay for itself) in two years.

Because Dr. Carroll was the most active in the enterprise, the partners made him the manager of the works. He supervised construction of the buildings, hired workers, and inspected the books kept by the company clerk. To save on transportation costs he employed an Annapolis shipwright to build a schooner of sixty tons burden. Other partners helped out by purchasing slaves and indentured servants, horses and wagons, shovels and axes. The furnace and outbuildings were completed by the end of 1732, and in 1734 the company made its first shipment of 292 tons of pig iron to England. Its sale of 716 tons the following year was 30 per cent of all the iron exported from Maryland and Virginia, which together produced 92 per cent of all the pig iron manufactured in America.

The Baltimore Ironworks was organized as an "iron plantation," modeled on a tobacco plantation. It mined the ore on its own lands and fired charcoal from its own forests. Its labor force, which numbered ninety-four by 1736, lived in company houses and purchased their necessities in a company store. A company farm raised corn for the workers and hay for the animals. "Country people" of the neighborhood brought beef, pork, and corn to the company store to exchange for tools and other imported goods. White laborers, some of them indentured servants, occupied the skilled positions: carpenter, sawyer, basket-maker, even a tailor. Black slaves, of whom there were forty-three in 1736, worked as miners, woodcutters, farm hands, and cooks. The slaves were evidently housed and fed in the same way as the other workers, but the details of their living conditions are not part of the written record.

The partners planned from the beginning to manufacture and sell bar iron, as well as pig iron, but British law proved a hindrance. Britain was happy to have the colonists producing pig iron, a "raw material" that required further refinement. But production of bar and wrought iron placed the colonies in direct competition with the politically powerful ironmasters of Britain. An iron act, part of the system of imperial trade regulations, imposed a high tariff on colonial bar iron imported into England. Both Tasker and Dr. Carroll sent letters to their London correspondents in an attempt to feel out the prospects for a change in the law. Dr. Carroll even wrote a pamphlet pointing out Britain's dependence on hostile Sweden (the two countries fought a brief war in 1718) for iron goods, and he sought to demonstrate that a subsidy for colonial iron would be to the mother country's advantage. Colonial production of bar iron, he contended, would not lead to the manufacture of tools and implements in America because the colonies had few artisans and their labor was "Extream Dear." Tasker, who was related to the Calverts by marriage, and Dulany, by then the Calverts' political servant, both sought to engage the proprietor in the cause of free trade for iron, but without success.

In 1734 Dr. Carroll traveled to England to make the company's case for free trade. It was precisely the wrong moment, for the British iron industry was then in a deep depression, due in part to a ban by Sweden on the import of finished iron goods. Unable to affect Swedish policy, British ironmasters were demanding further restrictions on colonial iron. Dr. Carroll wrote home bitterly in March 1735:

> There is no Carrying anything here without the force of money or aplycation of Politicks to answer tho never So consistent with reason. . . . Private Intrest here Renders the Plantations a Strange Raw Head and Bloody Bones as if all that hear talk of them were Children and to be frightened. By what I can collect in general you Stand a Poor Chance Unless things are better represented in your favor or indeed represented at all for I hear of no friend of consequence you have.

When the doctor entered politics two years later a professional agent retained in London to represent the interests of the colony was high on his agenda.

Although the empire continued to discriminate against colonial bar iron, there was a good market for it in America, as the number of craftsmen, particularly in New England and the middle colonies, increased steadily. The Baltimore Company was a financial success from its inception. Dr. Carroll bequeathed his fifth share of the company to his elder son, who in 1764 estimated the value at £10,000, with an annual return of £400 sterling. By that date the company had two forges for bar iron with a third under construction, 150 slaves, and 30,000 acres of land.

Wealth, status, and an interest in public affairs dictated Dr. Carroll's entry into politics. The lower house of the Maryland Assembly was still reeling from the proprietor's coup of 1733, when Lord Baltimore simultaneously reaffirmed his power to govern by edict and won the popular leader, Daniel Dulany, to his side. Through the mid-1730s the "Country Party" in the lower house struggled to preserve the gains it had made in the 1720s: the exclusion of the proprietor's executive appointees from the legislature and the publication of its proceedings. The *Votes and Proceedings* series, launched in 1731, was a printed journal of the lower house, showing how members voted on each roll call. It was aimed at keeping the voters informed on the issues that divided the colony, on the assumption that the Assembly's ultimate recourse against the autocracy of the proprietor was popular support. The *Maryland Gazette*, founded in 1726 under the editorship of William Parks, was the journalistic organ of the Country Party, and it made a point of keeping political issues before its readers.

Although the Country Party depended for support on the small and "middling" planters of the interior, its leadership was of the same social class as the proprietary element that controlled the council. Phillip Hammond and Stephen Bordley, who kept the legislative opposition afloat before Dr. Carroll appeared on the scene, possessed enormous wealth. Hammond was a tobacco planter/land speculator with 17,000 acres at his disposal, and Bordley was one of the most successful lawyers in the colony. The division between the "parties" in Maryland certainly involved economic issues, such as the impact of British trade regulations (and eventually British taxes), but the split was not a matter of rich versus poor. It was a matter of principle, ultimately, the principle of self-government.

Appropriations for arms and defense were one of the few powers allotted the Assembly, and hence one of its few sources of leverage. Since the 1670s the Assembly had imposed a duty on tobacco exports for defense expenditures in exchange for the proprietor's lifting of quitrents. However, this expired in 1733 when Lord Baltimore terminated all temporary laws. For the next few years the lower house approved duties only on an annual basis, in order to be assured of annual sessions. A dispute over procedure induced Governor Ogle to send the Assembly home prematurely in 1738, and, as a result, political lines were tightly drawn when the body convened the following year, when Dr. Carroll made his entry into politics.

Dr. Carroll won election to the lower house from the City of Annapolis in 1738 and immediately allied himself with the Country Party. His influence was soon evident. The lower house's response to the governor's annual message, normally a tepid reply, sharply criticized the "many recent instances of the people of this province being made a property to his lordship's officers and the many evils that proceed therefrom," including the fact that the people "are under the greatest apprehension of every act that may put them into their power or mercy." The house went on to object to the excessive fees charged by proprietary officials for land warrants, which discouraged settlers from coming to Maryland (significantly, an issue on which both wealthy speculators and penniless immigrants could agree).

Imminent war with Spain in 1739 gave the Assembly greater leverage. When Governor Ogle, supported by the Council, asked for added taxes for the purchase of arms and ammunition, the lower house tacked on to the bill an appropriation for a colonial agent in London. The bill died in a disagreement between the two houses, but not before the Assembly had issued a manifesto to "the people" and spread it across the pages of the *Votes and Proceedings*.

The manifesto challenged, for the first time, the proprietor's 1733 statement of prerogative. It named the proprietor as the enemy of the people and demanded an end to his special powers and financial privileges, except the privilege of collecting quitrents as landlord of the colony. Even these, declared the manifesto, ought to be subject to oversight by the Assembly in the interest of justice and fairness. Beneath the rhetoric lay the dawning notion of taxation by the consent of the governed, the principle that would underlie the American Revolution. For good measure, a copy of the address was sent to the king, and, as might have been expected, it received no response. There were no signatures to the documents approved by the Assembly, but the novel spirit with which it acted betrayed the mind and hand of Dr. Carroll.

The outbreak of war with Spain later in 1739 gave the lower house new bargaining power. It approved a supply bill for the British expedition to Cartagena, but it drew the funds from the license fees for taverns and ordinaries, a revenue that normally went to the proprietor. Governor Ogle had borne the brunt of the proprietor's unpopularity in these years, and by 1742 his influence had vanished. In that year the proprietor replaced him with Thomas Bladen, a native of Maryland and an in-law of the powerful Tasker family. Because the quarrel between executive and legislature was one of principle, rather than personalities, the change made little difference. Tensions heightened after Britain and France formally went to war in 1744, with "Bladen's Folly" and its general contractor, Patrick Creagh, becoming the symbolic victims. The proprietor reinstated Ogle as governor in 1747, but it made no difference. The vessel that carried Bladen back to England also bore a series of ten Assembly resolutions, which reiterated the demands of 1739, again with a copy to the king. Once more there was no royal response, but the Assembly's position was stronger than ever. And it had begun to lay a theoretical foundation for a new imperial constitution, one in which the role of the mother country and its agents, including the Lords Baltimore, was severely limited.

While the fighting between Britain and France, later referred to as the Old French War or King George's War (1744–48), strengthened the hand of the Assembly, it came near to ruining Dr. Carroll. By the early 1740s, before war was declared, Carroll had extended Annapolis's commercial hinterland to the Susquehanna River valley, where he was buying barrels of flour, fifty or more at a time, and sending them to London in his own vessels. His credit in London was such that he could threaten to transfer his custom to Glasgow if goods could not be obtained from English tradesmen of suitable quality and price. When he dispatched a vessel to his agent in Bridgetown, Barbados, Dr. Carroll instructed his shipmaster not to speak to any other vessel or touch any unauthorized port, except in an emergency. Unlike many colonial merchants, including his Annapolis friend, Patrick Creagh, Carroll was careful to remain within the law. He ordered his shipmaster not take on board contraband or prohibited goods of any kind that might subject the vessel or its cargo to forfeiture.

His caution brought him to near ruin after war was declared in 1744. He sought to continue business as usual, shipping tobacco and pig iron to London for bills of credit that were transmuted into consumer goods for his retail enterprise. Unfortunately, the fighting at sea caused a steep rise in insurance premiums, which ate up his profits and caused his bills of exchange to be dishonored. For perhaps the first time in his life he had to beg for leniency. "I am too old to run away," he told his London agent, "nor do I know well to Run to, the Rice trade is as bad as ours [referring to South Carolina] and I shall want more Cloaths if I go Northward[.] Therefore I hope you will contribute to keep me here a little longer till better times."

Despite the hard times of the mid-1740s, Carroll managed to finance a genteel English education for his elder son. He had taken Charles, then only eleven years old, to Europe with him in 1734. The younger Charles attended Eton, England's finest public (i.e. private) school, after which he entered Cambridge University. In his correspondence, in which Carroll invariably addressed his son as "My Dear Child," the doctor was full of fatherly advice. He gave the younger Charles a quarterly allowance of £5, plus extra sums when a series of special lectures was available. "This money," he wrote the youth of nineteen, "I hope you will lay out in Necessaries for your Person or Endowment of Your mind & not spend in wine or Riot. Remark, that Women & Wine are the Bane of Youth." The younger Charles returned to Maryland in 1746, perhaps because of his father's financial difficulties. He remained there until 1751 when he returned to London to study law at the Middle Temple of the Inns of Court.

In 1749 Dr. Carroll placed his younger son, Jacky, with a merchant in Philadelphia "to Acquire Knowledge in Mercantile Affairs." It was a pattern of paternal decision-making similar to that of Daniel Dulany. The eldest son was sent to England to learn the law and prepare for a career in politics; the younger son was trained to be a merchant. Carroll paid the Philadelphian £30 sterling a year plus board and lodging for on-the-job experience in the merchant's "Counting House." The apprenticeship lasted for three years during which, according to his father, Jacky "made good Progress in Surveying, Navigation, [and] the use of the Globe." After the young man completed "a Course of Merchants Accounts," Carroll brought him home in the fall of 1752 and settled him "at Patapsco," probably on or near the site of the future city of Baltimore. In the spring of 1753, Dr. Carroll wrote his older son, now in law school and addressed as "Dear Charles," that Jacky kept a "Batcheler's House" at Patapsco and that Carroll was building a flour mill and "Bakehouse" for him. By the fall of that year "Jacky" had become "John," had returned to Annapolis, and was suffering an "Intermitting Fever." He died in February 1754, and the father, feeling old and frail himself, sent an urgent message to his older son to return home. The younger Charles spent another year in London completing his legal studies.

In a letter to Charles in May 1754, Dr. Carroll estimated his own wealth at £10,000 sterling and £5,000 "current money" of Maryland. (A British pound sterling equaled about 1.6 pounds of Maryland currency.) He also estimated his son's estate (presumably passed to him in gifts) in lands, slaves, and livestock at £2,000 sterling. Noting that he himself was "past the Levity of Youth and wants no more than what may accommodate nature in moderation," Dr. Carroll predicted that most of his wealth would be passed on to his son. In that same letter he informed Charles that he was shipping 100 tons of pig iron to his agent in London, as well as a cargo of tobacco on Patrick Creagh's ship *Hanbury*. He asked his son to procure a £100 policy of insurance on the shipment, anticipating a premium of 2-1/2 per cent "(unless a

French war)." Clearly his business had recovered since the end of the Old French War in 1748. But, just as clearly, he anticipated a new outbreak of fighting. The first shot was in fact fired only a month later by a twenty-two-year-old Virginian, George Washington, who ambushed a party of Frenchmen in the valley of the Monongahela River. That conflict would go by the name of the French and Indian War (in Europe, the Seven Years' War).

In his letter of May 1754, Dr. Carroll noted that he was "infirm" and afflicted with "a violent cough," but he now left it to his son's "own judgment" as to when to return. His health continued to deteriorate, and he died on September 29, 1755. The younger Charles, having completed his legal studies, returned to Annapolis just a few weeks before his father's demise. Feeling a need to distinguish himself from the other Carrolls in town, he styled himself "Charles Carroll, Barrister." He took possession of his father's house on Church Street, a dwelling that was ever after known as the house of "the Barrister." He never practiced law, so far as we know, occupying himself with the management of his estate. He entered politics in the 1760s and, following in the footsteps of his father, promptly assumed leadership of the antiproprietary party. When the Revolution broke out in 1775, he was a member of the Council of Safety (the interim government) and of the convention that drafted the first state constitution. King George III was said to have grumbled that the American Revolution was provoked by "a brace of Adamses," referring to Samuel Adams and his cousin John of Massachusetts. Had the king directed his attention to the colony of Maryland, he might have been inclined to attribute the movement for independence to a trio of Carrolls, Dr. Carroll, his son, the Barrister, and their distant relative, Charles Carroll of Carrollton. Of the latter, more anon.

The house of Charles Carroll, Barrister, being moved in 1955 from its original location on the corner of Main and Conduit Streets to a site on the St. John's College Campus. *Historic Annapolis Foundation Collection.*

The house of Dr. Charles Carroll and his son, Charles Carroll, Barrister, as it stands today on the grounds of St. John's College. *Photo by author.*

The House of Charles Carroll the Barrister

The Barrister's own efforts at house-building, following his marriage in 1763, were directed at Mount Clare, on land his father had owned in Baltimore County (the house is the only colonial house now standing within the city limits of Baltimore City). The Annapolis house of Dr. Carroll and his son stood at the corner of Main and Conduit streets until 1955 when it was moved in order to make room for a fast-food restaurant. The structure found a home on the campus of St. John's College, facing King George Street, where today it provides administrative office space.

Charles Carroll of Carrollton. By Thomas Sully, completed in 1834. *Maryland Historical Society*

5

Charles Carroll of Carrollton: The Conservative as Revolutionary

The branch of the Carroll family that remained Catholic after arrival in Maryland had been ruined, as had Dr. Charles Carroll, by the seventeenth-century English confiscations in Ireland. The fortunes of this branch were quickly retrieved, however, in the New World. The first Charles Carroll ("the Settler") studied law at the Inns of Court and became a protégé of a cabinet minister in the government of James II. Through this connection he obtained a commission as attorney general of Maryland and sailed to the colony in the fateful year 1688. He lost his job almost immediately when Protestants seized control of Maryland and King William deprived the Lords Baltimore of their governing rights. The new Protestant regime instantly imposed disabilities on Catholics. They were deprived of the right to hold office, to practice law in certain courts, to worship publicly, or to educate their children in Catholic schools. The Settler thus faced many of the penal disabilities that had induced him to flee Ireland, but he never renounced his Catholic faith.

The Settler's strategy for achieving wealth was simple — he married well. In 1689 he married a wealthy widow who had inherited tobacco plantations and slaves from two previous husbands. When she died a year later in childbirth, Carroll became executor of her estate. He promptly opened a store and a warehouse on the home plantation in St. Mary's County. The Settler entered into two more marriages, each of which increased his fortune. In 1701 he settled in Annapolis, purchasing a tract of land on Spa Creek. He built a frame house on the site, which his son and grandson enlarged into the mansion visible today. By 1716 he owned a fourth of the town. In the meantime, The Settler managed to ingratiate himself with Charles Calvert, third Lord Baltimore, and in 1711 he received an appointment as judge and register of the proprietor's land office. In disposing of the proprietor's lands, Carroll seems to have been his own best customer, for when he died in 1720, he was the largest landowner in Maryland. He bequeathed to his sons, Charles and Daniel, estates totaling more than 47,000 acres on both the eastern and western shores of the colony.

His elder son, Charles Carroll of Annapolis, born in 1702, was educated in England and returned to Maryland in 1724. He seems to have inherited his father's genius for the acquisition of wealth and rapidly built upon his inheritance. He speculated in western lands, invested in the Baltimore Ironworks, and lent money to anyone with suitable credit. When he died in 1782 he was one of the wealthiest men in America. Carroll of Annapolis had two residences, a brick house linked to the Settler's frame house on Spa Creek, which he built in the 1720s, and a 10,000-acre tract called Doughoregan Manor in Baltimore (now Howard) County. When his son came of age, the "Annapolis" Carroll moved permanently to Doughoregan, where he built a sprawling three-story mansion.

On September 19, 1737, Carroll's first cousin, Elizabeth Brooke, gave birth to a son, whom the couple named Charles, after his father. He was the fifth of that name to reside in Annapolis and later would add "of Carrollton" to distinguish himself. The parents were not formally married, and we do not know how long they had been living together. Elizabeth Brooke first appears in the historical record three years earlier, at the age of twenty-five, when she served as a witness to the will of Carroll's brother, Daniel Carroll of Duddington. They would not be formally married until 1757 when their son was almost twenty years old. Neither Carroll of Annapolis nor Elizabeth ever explained the reason for this unusual domestic relationship. Historians have speculated that Carroll was hyper-cautious about preserving the fortune that he had so single-mindedly accumulated. Brooke came from a well-to-do family, but she had no property of her own. The speculation is that Carroll wished to prevent his property from falling into the hands of the Brooke family in the event of his own untimely death. Whatever the reason, Elizabeth Brooke seems to have gracefully accepted the arrangement, despite its obvious risks. Their formal wedding was preceded by a prenuptial agreement by which Elizabeth waived any rights to Carroll's property if she survived him and accepted instead an annual stipend of £100 sterling, a sum that was less that 10 per cent of Carroll's annual income.

Such arrangements may also have been dictated by Carroll's mistrust of the Protestant power structure of the colony. After the governance of Maryland was restored to the proprietor in 1715, the colony became subject to the English penal code, which repressed Catholics. They were not allowed to vote or hold public office. Catholics could attend school in Maryland only at the price of their faith, and they were not allowed to attend English schools. For elementary schooling Carroll sent his son to a Catholic mission on Bohemia Manor across the Chesapeake Bay where Jesuits conducted classes *sub rosa*. At the age of ten he was put on a ship, together with his second cousin, John Carroll (later to become America's first Catholic bishop), for schooling in France. He would remain in Europe for eighteen years; his mother would be dead by the time he returned.

The two Carrolls attended St. Omer College in Flanders, where English Jesuits provided instruction for the scions of English and American Catholic families. Charles studied philosophy and literature and became fluent in French. His father wrote frequent letters of advice on education, manners, and the composure of the "compleat gentleman." His mother wrote occasionally to inquire about his health and to remind him to take care of his teeth, but most of his correspondence was with his father. In 1754 the elder Carroll had occasion to chastise "Charley," as both parents called him: "You have not begun your Letters Dear *Papa & Mama*, as I formerly directed, nor Wrote to your Mother this year." The elder Carroll journeyed to Paris in 1757 to see his son give a public defense in French of a philosophic

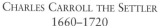

CHARLES CARROLL THE SETTLER
1660–1720

CHARLES CARROLL OF ANNAPOLIS
1702–1782

thesis. They spent happy days together discussing books and family matters, including marriage and inheritance. At his father's insistence, the younger Carroll would enter into a similar prenuptial agreement when he married.

Upon his father's departure, the younger Carroll went to Bourges in Flanders where he studied Roman and French civil law under a private tutor. After a grand tour of France, the Netherlands, and Germany he departed for London in 1759 to study English law. With an annual stipend from his father of £300, Carroll took up lodgings near the Inner Temple of the Inns of Court where his law instructor visited him. Equipped with a valet and a wardrobe that included twenty ruffled shirts, Carroll entered into the social life considered becoming of a future barrister (legal studies were ever secondary at the Inns of Court).

He remained, however, essentially American. Observing the English Parliament, where the Whig Party governed by the distribution of titles and favors, Carroll concluded that the political system, and the

CHARLES CARROLL OF CARROLLTON
1737–1832

Maryland Historical Society

society that underlaid it, was utterly corrupt. As he prepared to leave for home, he watched the House of Commons debate the Stamp Act and concluded that, ultimately, "America must become independent."

Upon landing in Annapolis, he discovered the problem created by his family's preference for the name "Charles" and immediately began signing his name, Charles Carroll of Carrollton. Carrollton was a family manor of 10,000 acres near the village of Frederick. The land was rented to tenants under the supervision of a steward. Carroll never lived there and rarely visited it.

Maryland, when Charles Carroll returned home in 1765, was in severe depression. The Seven Years' War had left the antagonists, Britain, France, and Germany, financially prostrate and debt-ridden. Tobacco imports to Europe virtually ceased, and the price plummeted. "Our trade is ruined," complained Benedict Calvert of Annapolis, "we are immensely in debt, and not the least probability of our getting clear." The unemployed, he reported, were roaming the highways, and the jails were "not half large enough" to accommodate those imprisoned for failing to pay debts. The hard times exacerbated the class conflict never far from the surface in Maryland society. Carroll, accustomed to the deference accorded the upper class in England, was disappointed in the attitude of Marylanders. He complained to an English friend that

> There is a mean, low dirty envy which creeps thro all ranks and cannot suffer a man a superiority of fortune, of merit, or of understanding in fellow citizens — either of these are sure to entail a general ill will and dislike upon the owner.

In this miasma of despair and bitterness landed Britain's effort to tax the colonies, the Stamp Act. The act required stamps to be placed on a variety of documents, including court papers, deeds and writs, ships' papers, and even newspapers. It thus had a direct impact on the most vocal groups in colonial society, lawyers, merchants, and journalists. Although the proceeds from the sale of stamps were earmarked for colonial military and naval defense, the act raised an important issue:

the power of Parliament to levy taxes within the colonies. Hitherto, taxes had been imposed by the colonial legislatures, bodies elected by the taxpayers. Taxation by Parliament was "taxation without representation."

Resistance to the act brought forth new popular leadership in nearly every colony, including Samuel Adams in Massachusetts, Patrick Henry in Virginia, and in Maryland, Samuel Chase. Like Patrick Henry, Chase was a spellbinding orator and self-trained lawyer who specialized in defending debtors. Artisans and tradesmen of Annapolis elected him to the lower house of the Assembly in 1764. The following year the merchants of Baltimore led the resistance to the Stamp Act in Maryland, organizing a chapter of the Sons of Liberty modeled on those of Boston and New York. Charles Carroll dismissed the Sons as "men of little note," but he admitted to an English friend that "Our political quarrels are now forgot or lay dormant while the dread of the Stamp Act continues and the common danger outweighs private concern." Although Parliament repealed the Stamp Act in 1766, Chase continued his rise to power. He and his followers won control of the Annapolis Common Council toward the end of that year and formed an alliance with the Baltimore Sons of Liberty.

Parliament provoked the colonists anew in 1767 with a set of excises on goods imported into the colonies (the Townshend Acts). The colonial response was a mercantile boycott, a refusal to import British goods. The nonimportation agreements began in the northern cities and spread gradually into the southern colonies. Maryland's reaction was tepid. The recovery of tobacco prices brought a general prosperity that lasted until 1770, and the colony's merchants were reluctant to enter a boycott that damaged retail sales. Baltimore City ultimately formed a nonimportation association at the urging of Philadelphia, but the agreement was never enforced.

Although he kept a close eye on the political scene, Charles Carroll of Carrollton did not become actively involved, due, no doubt, to the fact that he did not have the right to vote or hold public office. He took on some of the responsibility for managing his father's business affairs and resumed the search, begun in London, for a suitable mate. In tune with the penchant of the Maryland gentry for inbreeding, his choice was his first cousin (daughter of his mother's sister), Mary Darnall, known as Molly. Although the Darnalls were related to the proprietor, Molly's father, Henry Darnall, was a man of unpleasant disposition. Molly and her mother Rachel left him and moved into the household of Charles Carroll of Annapolis. Molly was only twelve years old at the time, and Rachel became the elder Carroll's house-keeper. Shortly thereafter Henry Darnall fled the colony with the law at his heels. He was executed a few years later in Nova Scotia. Rachel Darnall remained as housekeeper until her death in 1781. Whether the relationship went beyond that we do not know.

The elder Carroll treated Molly as a daughter, and she referred to him as "Papa." Although we don't know the details of her upbring-ing, he seems to have tutored her in reading and writing. The two of her letters that survive are written in a clear hand with, for the most part, proper spelling. Although Molly was quite attractive, if we are to believe Charles Willson Peale's portrait of her (1771), she did not immediately attract young Charley's attention when he returned from London. She was only fifteen at the time and twelve years younger than he.

In 1766, the younger Carroll became betrothed to his mother's twenty-three-year-old cousin, Rachel Cooke, but wedding plans were terminated by the young woman's sudden and untimely death. In the midst of his grief, Carroll took notice of Molly Darnall, now eighteen. In August 1767 he informed an English friend that he had won "the affections of a young lady endowed with every quality to make me happy in the married state: virtue, good sense & good temper." Papa was delighted and stoutly maintained that he had done nothing to fur-ther the match. The one obstacle was the Carrolls' insistence on a prenuptial agreement to protect the family fortune in the event Molly survived Charles. Molly was satisfied with the offer of £300 sterling a year in lieu of dower; the problem was that, as a minor, she could not legally enter into such a contract. In the end it required a special "enabling act" to be passed by the legislature and signed by the governor. The wedding took place at last on June 5, 1768. "She brings no dowry," Charles wrote his English friend, "but she is of good family, beautiful, sweet-tempered, virtuous and sensible."

The elder Carroll and Rachel Darnall had by this time moved to Doughoregan, and Molly enthusiastically undertook the refurbishing of the house on Spa Creek. By 1770 the miserly senior Carroll was protesting the purchases of furniture and other "superfluities." His letter concluded: "What is decent & Convenient, You ought to Have, there is no end to a desier for finery of any sort. The Sumpuousity of Princes leaves room for desier, I wish Yours and Mollys to be governed by Reason. Be content with what is neat Clean & Necessary."

The Stamp Act began the process by which the Country Party in Maryland gradually refocused itself, from resistance to proprietary authority to resistance to Parliament. The colony nevertheless watched with seeming detachment as New England, led by Boston, marched inexorably toward revolution: occupation by British troops (1768), the Boston Massacre (1770), and the Boston Tea Party (1773). The only excitement in Maryland during these momentous times was a controversy over fees charged by proprietary officials, a revival of an issue now almost a half-century old. Although a matter of only local concern, the fee controversy gave birth to a revolutionary "Popular Party," and it brought Charles Carroll of Carrollton to the center stage of Maryland politics.

The root of the fee controversy lay in the tobacco inspection system, initiated by the legislature in 1747 to improve the quality and reputation of Maryland tobacco. To secure approval of the act, the proprietor had allowed the legislature to set the fees that proprietary officials charged for tobacco inspection services. When the inspection act came up for renewal in 1769, the lower house seized the opportunity to make an issue of other fees charged by certain executive officers and of the practice of allowing offices to be bought and sold. They complained that a person who purchased an office was obliged to enhance his fees in every way possible in order to recoup his investment.

An inquiry the following year revealed that Daniel Dulany, as deputy secretary of the colony, made from £1,000 to £1,500 annually from fees, and his brother, Walter, reaped only a little less from his office as commissary general. The lower house accordingly passed an act regulating officials' fees and prohibiting the sale of proprietary offices. The act was directed specifically at the Dulanys, both of whom were members of the upper house. When the upper house rejected the bill, the Assembly passed a series of resolutions, which were printed and distributed to the public. The resolutions accused the Dulanys and the land office judges of conducting their offices in an "illegal and oppressive" manner. Prior to this time the members of the lower house had been, as Charles Carroll of Annapolis noted, "in awe of Dulany," afraid to criticize him for fear of having their own aspirations for office wrecked. The Assembly's newfound fortitude reflected the spirit of the times, the self-confidence that stemmed from the resistance to taxes under the Stamp Act and the Townshend Acts.

Governor Robert Eden, who had arrived in the colony in 1769, allowed himself to become embroiled in the dispute. He sent the Assembly home and five days later reestablished the fee schedule by proclamation. He then called for a new election in hopes of getting a more moderate house. The fee issue was thus placed directly before the public, and the election resulted in a lower house more angry and intransigent than ever. After an exchange of strongly worded letters with the governor in the session of 1771, the delegates approved by a vote of thirty-one to three a resolution labeling the governor's fee proclamation "robbery." The upper house prevented any legislative regulation of fees, and the tobacco inspection system languished. A plunge in tobacco prices forced the two houses to compromise in 1773 in order to bring tobacco exports under qualitative control, and the controversy subsided.

At that juncture a newspaper war broke out that rejuvenated the movement for independence. An election was scheduled for the spring of 1773, pursuant to the colony's charter, because there had been a change in proprietor. Frederick, the sixth Lord Baltimore, had died, and the province had come into the possession of his illegitimate son, Henry Harford. Daniel Dulany, hoping to convince the electorate to return a more moderate lower house, published a clever dialogue in the *Maryland Gazette* on January 7, 1773. The protagonists were "First Citizen," an opponent of the governor's fee proclamation, and "Second Citizen," who gave reasonable responses to all the criticisms. In the end, "First Citizen" saw the error of his ways and promised to vote against the "designing faction of men" who wanted to destroy the colony.

Dulany's thrust called for a response, and Charles Carroll of Carrollton seized the opportunity. The two families had been feuding for some years. In the late 1760s, Charles Carroll of Annapolis had accused the Dulanys of fiddling with the accounts of the Baltimore Iron Works. (Walter Dulany was in charge of the company books.) The elder Carroll threatened legal action, which served as a counterweight to a suit the Dulanys had been pursuing for several years claiming damages against Carroll for illegally charging compound interest. In 1768, just prior to the younger Carroll's marriage, the dispute had degenerated into a juvenile exchange between Walter Dulany and the younger Carroll in which Dulany suggested a gunfight "in a private place." He taunted Carroll for his diminutive size (he stood only five feet, eight inches) and puny physique. Carroll replied that he would ride down a certain road the following morning armed with pistols. He did not relish a fight, and, indeed, made out his will before taking the ride. To his relief, Dulany, all bluster himself, never made an appearance.

In addition to his personal reasons for challenging Daniel Dulany in January 1773, Carroll had political motives. He had joined a circle of men active in the opposition to the proprietary: Chase, William Paca, and Thomas Johnson, all lawyers of Annapolis. Lacking the right to vote or run for office, Carroll could advance his standing in this group only through the public prints. Writing under the name "First Citizen" on February 4, Carroll advanced historical and legal arguments to demonstrate that Governor Eden's fee proclamation was arbitrary and invalid. Dulany replied under the pseudonym "Antilon," and the exchange went on for six months. The public soon recognized the identity of the two contestants and clearly sided with Carroll. William

Paca and Mathias Hammond, who represented the city of Annapolis in the lower house, published a congratulatory address to "First Citizen." Sensing defeat, Dulany sought to appeal to the latent religious bigotry in the colony. "Who is this citizen?," he asked. A person, he answered, who is distrusted by the law "on account of his principles" and is disabled from participating in an election. "He is not a Protestant," Dulany declared, implying that Carroll lacked even the right to voice an opinion on public questions. To the query "Who is this citizen?," Carroll answered: "A man . . . of an independent fortune, one deeply interested in the prosperity of his country, a friend of liberty, a settled enemy to lawless prerogative." Carroll declined to enter a dispute about the rights of Catholics, citing instead a Latin motto which translated as "We remember, and forgive."

In the course of the spring, through meetings at the Carroll house and elsewhere, the opposition to the governor and proprietary officials gradually coalesced. By early May, on the eve of the Assembly election, opponents referred to themselves as the "Popular Party." At the core of the group were Charles Carroll, Barrister, and his father-in-law, Matthew Tilghman, long-standing leaders of the Country Party. Tilghman was a wealthy planter from Talbot County with a talent for political organization. Also in the group were Charles Carroll of Carrollton's new-found lawyer friends, Chase, Paca, and Johnson, the latter being the personal attorney for Carroll's father. Chase had close ties with Baltimore City merchants, and the ideology of "First Citizen" cemented them to the new party. In the election the Popular Party won control of the lower house. When the legislative session opened, Chase, Johnson, Paca, and Tilghman received the most prestigious committee assignments. The Popular Party had a broader horizon than the old Country Party, and in the fall of 1773 the lower house created a committee of correspondence to exchange ideas with revolutionary leaders in other colonies. Chase, Johnson, Paca, and Tilghman were all named to the committee.

Carroll in the meantime had been working steadily to improve the house on Spa Creek. The grounds by 1770 contained an orchard, a walled garden, outbuildings, and a stable. He enlarged the link with the original frame house (where, until recently, his grandmother had been living) with an arched brick passageway. He then turned his attention to the garden, the space bounded by the house, Spa Creek, and Duke of Gloucester Street. Showing his European training, he walled the garden into a 3-4-5 triangle, a figure favored by French landscape designers, and built a stone seawall along Spa Creek (the "4" leg of the triangle, the Duke of Gloucester Street being the hypotenuse or "5" leg). He later constructed two "pleasure pavilions" on the seawall and a carriage house on the far side of Duke of Gloucester Street. To give an illusion of space he built terraces into the descending garden. The terraces increased in width, from thirty feet at the apex of the triangle, to forty feet, and ultimately to fifty feet in width. The optical effect was to bring Spa Creek and its maritime activity closer to the house, while the eye's widening periphery conveyed a sense of breathing space.

Carroll's vivacious wife Molly thoroughly enjoyed the Annapolis social scene. The provincial capital was by then a social center of some importance. The town's French hairdresser was in demand, as women wore the high headdresses fashionable in England. Clothing, imported from the mother country, was also in the latest London fashion. The tables of the rich were adorned with silver plate and cut glass, and featured the choicest wines and delicacies. A proprietary customs collector effused in 1770:

> I am persuaded there is not a town in England of the same size as Annapolis, which can boast a greater number of fashionable and handsome women, and were I not satisfied to the contrary, I should suppose that the majority of our belles possessed every advantage of a long and familiar intercourse with the manners and habits of London.

In this society Molly Carroll moved with charm and social grace. On one occasion she deflected without offense an indelicate advance on the part of Governor Eden, a notorious woman-chaser. Molly's mother reported the incident to Carroll's father, and it added a personal note to the family's growing rift with the governor, the proprietor, and even the English Parliament.

The Carroll House as it appeared in the late nineteenth century after the Redemptorist Fathers attached it to St. Mary's Church and rectory. *Maryland Historical Society.*

As so often happened in the eighteenth century, Molly's health was ultimately wrecked by excessive child-bearing. In the seven years after her marriage, she suffered one miscarriage and gave birth to four children. Only two survived: Mary, born in 1770, and a son, inevitably named Charles, born in 1774. Although the entire family was elated with the birth at last of a son and heir, Molly was not allowed to retire from childbearing. In the next six years she had three more children, all but one of whom died in infancy.

As events spun toward revolution, Charles Carroll of Carrollton intensified his desire for an "honest fame" and a leadership role. The Boston Tea Party provoked the British Parliament into passing punitive legislation that the colonists promptly labeled "intolerable acts." The laws imposed military rule on the Massachusetts colony, and they closed the port of Boston until the city paid for the lost tea. The colonial response was a call, emanating from Virginia and echoing throughout the colonies, for a Continental Congress to meet in Philadelphia in September 1774.

In Maryland the pressure of events created a fissure in the Popular Party. Charles Carroll, despite his conclusion a decade earlier that America must some day become independent, did not want a complete break with the mother country, at least not before Marylanders could devise a government to replace it. Mistrustful of the lower classes and their appetites, Carroll abhorred a governmental vacuum. Paca, Chase, Tilghman, and the Barrister felt the same way. Accordingly, they were willing to compromise with the governor on the matter of officials' fees, and their initial reaction to the intolerable acts was one of restrained concern. Such moderation alienated a small group of firebrands in the assembly led by John Hall and the Hammond brothers, Mathias and Rezin, all three Anne Arundel County planters.

The schism surfaced at a public meeting in Annapolis on May 25, 1774, called to consider a request by the Boston committee of correspondence for an intercolonial nonimportation and nonexportation pact. Carroll, Chase, and Paca attempted to control the meeting, but they were soon outshouted by the Hammonds and Hall. Each side then attempted to outdo the other in denouncing British policy, and the result was the passage of a resolution calling on all lawyers to cease prosecuting suits for debts owed to British creditors while the Boston Port Act remained law. The Annapolitans' resolve had broad appeal because nearly every Maryland planter owed money to a British merchant.

This victory for the Hall-Hammond faction, however, was only temporary. The Annapolis meeting also called for the election of a convention with representatives of each county to choose Maryland's delegates to the Continental Congress. Because such an election was not authorized by the governor, it was outside of English law and hence not subject to the penal restrictions on Catholics. Accordingly, when the Maryland convention met on June 22, 1774, Charles Carroll of Carrollton proudly took his seat as a delegate from Annapolis. The Popular Party moderates controlled the convention that met in Annapolis, and the delegation dispatched to Philadelphia consisted of Chase, Paca, Tilghman, and Robert Goldsborough (an Eastern Shore planter). Although not officially a delegate to Congress, Carroll traveled to Philadelphia on his own initiative. He was not allowed to attend the sessions of the Congress, which were conducted behind closed doors, but he kept abreast of the debates through the whirl of evening social activities that followed the meetings.

The Congress was divided in opinion in much the same way as Maryland. Radicals from Virginia and Massachusetts, though unwilling as yet to contemplate independence, favored a strong protest to the king and preparation for armed conflict. Moderates, mostly from the middle colonies, hoped to preserve the empire, but with better balance and more American influence. Despite his own conservatism, Carroll found himself in general agreement with the Virginians and the New Englanders. He supported the declaration of grievances that was sent to England and the Congress's call for a continental association barring the importation of British goods.

Carroll was back in Annapolis by September 29, and hence seems to have missed the most radical move by the Continental Congress: the call upon the colonies to arm themselves for self-defense. Given this encouragement, the towns of New England began organizing militia units ("Minute Men") and stockpiling arms and gunpowder. Throughout the winter of 1774–75 the British army in Boston undertook periodic forays into the interior searching for the arms caches. One such expedition to Lexington and Concord in April 1775 provoked a gunfight that launched the Revolution.

In the course of the winter the Maryland convention evolved into a semi-permanent legislature. The Popular Party remained in control and sent a delegation of familiar faces to the Second Continental Congress in May 1775. Although Governor Eden was still in the colony (the Popular leaders, still in hopes of a reconciliation, refused to let him leave), his authority was nil. Sensing the need for an executive, the convention created a Council of Safety in July 1775. On it were the usual Popular leaders plus, for the first time, Charles Carroll. He had won public office at last, and he stood as a symbol of one of the first and finest achievements of the Revolution, religious toleration.

The function of the Council of Safety was public security: defense against any military threat from abroad and the maintenance of law and order at home. Every revolution carries an implicit threat of anarchy, and Charles Carroll was not alone in fretting about the security of his property. One merchant who had sold goods on credit told the convention gloomily that "the private animosity of some men render my property insecure and bring my family into the utmost terror." Debtors refused to meet their obligations, and some reckless souls broke into jails and freed persons who had been taken into custody for defaulting on their payments. The Eastern Shore was of particular concern to the Council of Safety because it had a large number of landless tenant farmers who were indifferent to a revolution promulgated by the landed gentry. In the past decade the Methodist movement had made substantial progress in those counties, and converts tended to be loyal to their English founder, John Wesley. Eastern Shore loyalists were a source of concern throughout the Revolution.

Apprehension blossomed into near-hysteria in November 1775 when Virginia's Royal Governor Lord Dunmore offered freedom to all slaves and indentured servants who would respond to his banner and take up arms for the king. The fear of slave insurrection was ever-present in the southern colonies, particularly in areas like the lower Eastern Shore, where blacks were a significant portion of the population. The fear was not unfounded. A Dorchester County committee of inspection reported that "malicious and imprudent speeches of some among the lower classes of whites" had induced black slaves to believe that the king's troops would set them free. The committee had seen fit to disarm all blacks, and it had collected some eighty guns, bayonets, and swords. By the end of 1775, Charles Carroll of Carrollton, who had written as recently as September of his happy anticipation that the imperial crisis would be "decided by arms," was having second thoughts. His father wrote to him in December that social disorder made it essential to "establish a government. The convention must say what sort of one. Rogues and enemies must be punished. Nothing essential to the general safety can be done as things are now."

Thoughts about government were momentarily shelved in the spring of 1776 when the Continental Congress placed Carroll on a commission to induce Canada to become the fourteenth colony in rebellion. A military conquest of Canada had come within an eyelash of success in 1775. An army formed by the Continental Congress and commanded by Richard Montgomery had invaded Canada by way of Lake Champlain and seized Montreal, while another army under General Benedict Arnold had passed through the wilderness of Maine and descended on Quebec. The assault on Quebec on New Year's Eve failed when Montgomery was killed and Arnold wounded. The Americans maintained possession of Montreal, however, and Congress hoped that the Canadians, most of whom were French, would join the American cause.

Carroll was placed on the commission because of his religion, as was his cousin, John Carroll, by now the most prominent Catholic priest in Maryland, and perhaps in all British America. Both were instructed to assure the French Catholic population of Canada that Congress would guarantee its freedom of religion. Benjamin Franklin and Samuel Chase were put on the commission as members of

Charles Carroll is seated at the far right in this engraving, *Congress Voting Independence, July 1776*, by Edward Savage, 1796. *The National Portrait Gallery, Smithsonian Institution.*

Congress. Carroll journeyed to Philadelphia, and the party proceeded by carriage to New York. Carroll described Franklin as "a most enjoying and entertaining companion of sweet, even lively temper, full of facetious stories" that always ended with a moral. From New York the party went by boat up the Hudson River and down the lakes to Montreal. There they met General Arnold, whose energy convinced Carroll that he was destined for military greatness.

The mission was doomed to failure. The Quebec Act, adopted by Parliament in 1774, had extended religious toleration to British Canada, and the resident population had no wish to exchange one

Protestant, English-speaking master for another. A detachment of soldiers that Arnold had left outside Quebec throughout the winter as a sort of symbolic siege fled as soon as the British emerged from the citadel in the spring. When reinforcements arrived from England, the British took the offensive, and Arnold himself was forced to abandon Montreal and retreat southward to Lake Champlain.

Franklin, bothered by boils on his legs, returned home in early May, and John Carroll accompanied him. Charles Carroll and Chase stayed on because Congress had given them supervisory authority over military operations in the north. They started south in early June after Arnold evacuated Montreal, arriving in Philadelphia on June 11. In Congress the general feeling was that Carroll and Chase had done as much as it was possible for men to do, under the circumstances. John Adams, who chaired the Congress's board of war, was impressed with Carroll's report and hinted to Maryland leaders that Charles Carroll ought to be added to the colony's delegation.

In the fall of 1775 the Maryland convention, reflecting the conservatism of the Popular Party, instructed its congressional delegation to resist all efforts to declare a national independence. Attitudes in Maryland on the question began to shift in the spring of 1776, influenced in part by Thomas Paine's pamphlet *Common Sense*. Both Chase and Carroll returned from Canada ardent advocates of independence. The mission convinced them that Britain would never make the concessions necessary to induce the colonists to remain within the empire. Both attended county meetings that instructed the convention to change its instructions to the congressional delegation. The convention did so, voting in favor of independence on June 28.

Congress, in the meantime, was entertaining a resolution in favor of independence offered by Virginia's Richard Henry Lee, and it had named a committee to draft a Declaration. It approved Thomas Jefferson's draft on July 4, and that same day the Maryland convention elected Carroll a congressional delegate. Signing of the Declaration of Independence was delayed until August 2 because delegates from Pennsylvania and New York had to await instructions. Carroll took his seat on July 18. The following day he had the satisfaction of voting in favor of having the document engrossed. A pretty story became part of Maryland mythology in the course of the nineteenth century: that on the signing day, August 2, after Hancock and Franklin had joked about hanging together or hanging separately, Carroll added "of Carrollton" to his name so British authorities would know which Charles Carroll was the rebel. The reality is that Carroll had been signing his name "of Carrollton" since returning from Europe a decade earlier.

Congress, at the request of John Adams, added Carroll to the board of war, a committee that had supervisory authority over the Continental Army and its commander, George Washington. Although this body would become crucially important a year later when, after a string of military defeats, Washington became the target of congressional criticism, its powers were ill-defined in 1776. Carroll, as a result, was able to divide his time between Philadelphia and Annapolis. Maryland required his attention. Independence, all along, had been linked in his mind with the formation of a state government. But not just any government. For several years the colony's orators and newspaper contributors had founded the opposition to Great Britain on the will of the people. But Carroll and other popular leaders did not want this message to be taken literally. They wanted an orderly society governed by the rich and the publicly spirited, in short, by themselves.

When, on July 3, the Maryland convention issued a call for an election of delegates to a constitutional convention, it specified that the

property requirements for voting of the proprietary era (fifty acres of land or a "visible estate" of £40) were to remain in effect. This reflected the eighteenth-century view that voting was not a right but a privilege, one extended only to those who had a "stake in society" and thus something to lose by errant political behavior. Nevertheless, such was the democratic spirit that had been aroused by revolutionary oratory that judges in five counties ignored the instruction and allowed all taxpayers to vote. Although the judges in Anne Arundel County enforced the property qualification, the Hammonds still managed to cause trouble. Shortly after the polls opened, Rezin Hammond addressed the assemblage and declared that every man that bore arms in defense of his country had a right to vote, and if they were deprived of the right, they had no obligation to bear arms in the fighting. In the ensuing mêlée non-resident soldiers who happened to be camped in the county demanded the right to vote. The judges had to close the polls for a time to restore order. In the end the county divided its vote, sending Hammond and one of his allies to the convention, along with Chase and Charles Carroll, Barrister. Charles Carroll of Carrollton, rejected by the voters of the county, won a seat in the convention as a delegate from Annapolis. Allowing a person to represent any city or county in which he owned property was one of the many features of the old régime that guaranteed control by the gentry.

As a result, the composition of the convention that met in Annapolis in August was not to the Popular Party's liking. But its leaders need not have worried. They seized control of the meeting and dominated the proceedings. They were able to do so, in part, because of their legislative experience. Most of the men elected in the counties that had expanded the suffrage had never served in a legislative body. The committee named to draft a constitution consisted of the old Popular Party leadership, including Charles Carroll of Carrollton. The document that emerged from this committee was one of the most conservative in America. It reflected the eighteenth-century concern — one certainly shared by Charles Carroll — for balanced government, that is, the balance of power and interest between the wealthy few and the debt-ridden many.

The upper house of the Maryland legislature, or Senate, was envisioned as the guardian of the interests of the élite. A property qualification of £1,000 current money restricted its membership to the modern equivalent of millionaires. The Senate was further insulated from popular influence by indirect election; its members were chosen, not by the voters, but by a specially elected electoral college, a device that was unique among revolutionary state constitutions. The lower house, or House of Delegates, in theory represented the interests of the multitude, but its members were required to possess an estate worth £500 current money. The electorate was restricted to persons with fifty acres of land or a "visible estate" of £30, requirements that only about half of the adult male population could meet. These qualifications on voting and officeholding ensured that the new state would be controlled by the planter class.

Although Carroll shuddered at every amendment proposed by the Hammond element in the convention, the only important changes were a reduction in the term of senators from seven years to four and of the delegates from three years to one. This meant annual elections, which Carroll thought could have disastrous consequences. Significantly, none of the changes proposed by the democratic element in the convention struck at the basic structure of the proposed government. And it was not for lack of models because reformers had the upper hand in several other states. Georgia and Pennsylvania both experimented with a one-house legislature, and Pennsylvania extended the suffrage to all white male taxpayers. New Jersey even allowed blacks and women to vote. The Maryland constitution ensured indefinite control of the state by the planter class.

Neither Carroll nor any of the other Popular Party leaders were confident of control in 1776–77, however. The Eastern Shore was still in a state of near anarchy. In early 1777, recruiting efforts in Baltimore County sparked riots that quickly involved servants and slaves. The decision by British General Sir William Howe in July 1777 to attack Philadelphia by way of Chesapeake Bay, with a landing at Elkton, was seen in Maryland as an effort to divide the state in two. To some extent it did, as Eastern Shore loyalists flocked to Howe's standard, and their knowledge of the countryside helped him defeat George Washington at the Battle of the Brandywine.

Although Popular Party leaders controlled the first state legislature that met in February 1777, they arrived in Annapolis with deep foreboding about their own future and that of the Revolution. Accordingly they embarked over the next two years on a program to popularize their leadership and the revolutionary cause. It was at great cost to themselves in the short term, but the reward was a successful Revolution and control of the state in the long run. Their first move was tax reform. The proprietary régime had taxed Marylanders through rents and fees; the only tax imposed by the colonial assembly was a poll tax, a "head" tax on individuals which fell equally on rich and poor. In October 1777 the legislature imposed a graduated property tax, which fell doubly hard on the wealthy. In addition, it taxed slaves, pig iron, and household plate. Carroll accepted the new taxes because he thought they were essential to the success of the Revolution.

Next, the legislature decided to finance its military effort by issuing paper money. This was hardly unusual; every state, as well as the Continental Congress, financed the Revolution with paper money. It was a form of public finance that we would now call "defense bonds." However, because the states had neither gold nor sufficient tax authority to back the paper, it depreciated rapidly. To shore it up the Maryland Assembly made the money legal tender for the payment of debts, and this was another self-inflicted wound for the élite. Men like Charles Carroll and his father, who had lent money in sterling or its equivalent, were now repaid in worthless paper. Carroll disliked the law but accepted it resignedly as "the price of Revolution."

Although Carroll was elected to the first Maryland Senate, he retained his seat in the Continental Congress. As a result, between 1777 and 1779 he divided his time among Philadelphia, York, Pennsylvania (the seat of Congress after the British captured Philadelphia), and Annapolis. His father continued to manage their business affairs, while complaining loudly of the legal tender law. That left Molly solely responsible for the family (another daughter, Anne Brooke Carroll had been born on October 30, 1776, but died in 1778). She moved with the children to Doughoregan, probably because, with the British prowling the Chesapeake, it was considered safer. In addition to assuming responsibility for the children's education, she shouldered the numerous responsibilities of the plantation mistress. She supervised a weaving operation that evidently made cloth for soldiers. She ordered from Carroll's agent in London medicine and a variety of household goods, and, at her husband's request, she arranged for a transition of overseers at Doughoregan.

Molly's father-in-law, Charles Carroll of Annapolis, spent much of his waning energy (he died in 1782) in public denunciation of the legal tender law. This developed into a rift between the Carrolls and Samuel Chase. Chase, like other smalltime lawyers and merchants of Baltimore and Annapolis, had sought to enrich himself by wartime speculation in lands and goods. He had gone deeply into debt and naturally found relief in the legal tender act. When the elder Carroll discovered that Chase, who had been elected to the House of Delegates, was profiting from his legislative votes, he denounced him as a "scoundrel" who merited "the coarsest and most opprobrious epithets which can be put on paper." When Chase replied that he cared not for the elder Carroll's questioning of his honor, he was answered with "neither does a whore."

The younger Carroll strove hard to maintain a cordial relationship with Chase, who had a large following in the countryside. Carroll even intercepted and destroyed some of his father's more ferocious letters. The political scene calmed considerably in 1778 when the British retired to New York City and peace returned to the Chesapeake. In 1780 the Assembly quietly repealed the legal tender act, and the following year Maryland ratified the Articles of Confederation, allowing the first attempt at a national union to go into effect. Carroll had already given up his seat in Congress so he could concentrate more on his family and business.

The family required a good deal of attention. Carroll had moved Molly, the children, and the servant staff of twenty back to Annapolis in 1778 when the war moved northward. Molly was now chronically ill, suffering from headaches and nausea. Her father-in-law thought that she had become addicted to opium through the chronic use of laudanum. She occasionally went to the baths of Virginia for a cure, but the respites were only temporary. After two-year-old Anne Brooke Carroll died in 1778, Molly had given birth to another daughter, Catherine.

Charles Carroll of Annapolis made out a will in June 1780 that bequeathed his entire estate to his son. There was little left in the way of currency. The elder Carroll had outstanding loans of £24,230 sterling at the beginning of the war. Most of those debts had been repaid in worthless paper. But he still had a total of 40,000 acres of Maryland land, most of it rented to tenants, plus the annual income from the Baltimore Iron Works. About that time he returned to the Annapolis house, probably to be with his son and daughter-in-law, to whom he was much attached. He died on May 30, 1782, and Molly followed him to the grave only eleven days later.

Peace commissioners reached a provisional agreement in November 1782, and on April 11, 1783, Congress issued a proclamation ending hostilities on land and sea. Annapolis greeted the occasion with a huge celebration. A structure capable of accommodating several thousand people was erected on "Carroll's Green" (probably at the foot of Duke of Gloucester Street), and the capitol building was turned into a candlelit ballroom. Having been chased from Philadelphia by army mutineers in 1781, Congress had moved to Princeton and then, in November 1783, to Annapolis. Washington journeyed there in December to resign his commission in the army. Carroll was on a committee that presented him with an address from the Maryland Assembly. A painting of the scene by Jonathan Trumbull, who had been an aide to Washington during the war, shows thirteen-year-old Polly and five-year-old Catherine standing next to their father in the Assembly hall.

A postwar depression which struck the new nation in 1784 brought new turmoil to Maryland politics. In the House of Delegates Samuel

Chase sponsored a new paper money bill with the avowed purpose of debtor relief. Led by Carroll, the Senate rejected the measure, and the deadlock between the two houses lasted for two years. In September 1786 a convention gathered in Annapolis to consider ways of strengthening the Articles of Confederation. The convention, attended by the leading nationalists of the day, James Madison and Alexander Hamilton, met in the state capitol. The Maryland legislature had gone home that spring without even bothering to nominate a delegate. Chase was suspicious of a central government that might be hostile to debtor relief. Carroll, his eyes focused on state politics, failed to understand the intentions of Madison and Hamilton. The Annapolis gathering concluded with a proposal to elect yet another convention, in Philadelphia the following May, to consider changes in the confederation.

In the spring of 1787 the Maryland Assembly named five men to attend the meeting in Philadelphia. Both Carroll and Chase were placed on the delegation. Each declined to serve. Chase, who was probably aware of the creditor orientation of the leaders of the reform movement, Hamilton and Madison, had no interest in a strong central government. Carroll, it has long been thought, declined to go because he was afraid to leave Chase alone in the Assembly. However, prosperity had returned to the state, and paper money had not even been mentioned that spring. It seems more likely that Carroll, who had not communicated with any of the leaders of the movement for federal reform, even George Washington, was simply struck by the fear of change, a reluctance to tinker with a government that seemed to work reasonably well.

When the new Constitution was published in September 1787, however, Carroll gave it his hearty support. Chase's worst fears were confirmed, for the Constitution prohibited the states from interfering with contracts (i.e., by debtor relief legislation) or making anything other than gold or silver legal tender. Chase and his followers noisily opposed ratification of the document. However, the old Popular Party leaders were still in control, and Maryland ratified the Constitution by a margin of two to one. Carroll agreed to serve as United States

Senator in the First Congress. He loyally supported the policies of President Washington, but he otherwise had no impact on the formation of the new government. He left the Senate in 1792 a confirmed Federalist, horrified by the violence of the French Revolution and hostile to the pro-French party of Thomas Jefferson.

Much of Carroll's energy was devoted to the house on Spa Creek in the 1790s. He changed the appearance to give it more of a "Georgian" look in keeping with the times. The roof installed by his father had been hipped in the Dutch colonial style (like Patrick Creagh's house). That was torn off and a third story added to the house (fourth story if one counts the ground floor kitchen). The chimneys were enlarged, and the new roof had gables for windows. The added story was a single room, which probably served as a chapel for the Catholic community of Annapolis. (The Carrolls maintained a family priest at both Doughoregan and Annapolis.) Carroll also enlarged the bay between the two houses and installed a library on the second floor of the bay.

His son Charles, who had been sent to Europe in 1785 for education in Catholic institutions, returned to Maryland in 1799. The following year he married Harriet Chew, daughter of the chief justice of Pennsylvania. Carroll's wedding present was a gift of land, later incorporated into Baltimore City, and the construction of a mansion. Completed in 1801 in the "Federal style," the structure was given the name "Homewood." It remains today a graceful presence on the grounds of the Johns Hopkins University.

Less than a year later daughter Catherine married Robert Goodloe Harper, U.S. Senator from South Carolina. Harper was an arch-Federalist and author of the infamous Sedition Act of 1798. Carroll initially opposed the match, not because of Harper's politics, but because the South Carolinian was debt-ridden, due to speculation in western lands. Carroll was ultimately brought around by the intercession of Richard Caton, Mary's husband. After the wedding the Harpers moved to Baltimore City where the erstwhile senator opened a successful law practice.

Carroll's final foray into politics occurred in 1800 when he spoke out in favor of the election of John Adams over Thomas Jefferson. A

Republican newspaper noted his appearance when he visited his Carrollton estate in Frederick County:

> Even old Charles Carroll, that hoary-headed aristocrat, has gone
> down to the Manor, no doubt with a view to influence the tenants
> on that place. Shall the people be dictated to by this lordly nabob
> because he has more pelf than some others? Has he more virtue,
> more honor, more honesty than a good industrious farmer? Dares
> he with his British monarchical and aristocratic policies, come into
> Frederick County to cajole, to swindle the people out of their
> rights? Is he, old in iniquity as he is, to be the chief director of the
> people on the Manor? Citizens of Frederick County, set Charles
> Carroll at defiance!

Carroll was clearly out of place in the dawning age of democracy. His public activities for the remainder of his life were symbolically linked to his signing of the Declaration of Independence. He declined, giving reasons of health, invitations from both New York and Washington, D.C., to attend celebrations of the fiftieth anniversary of the Declaration of Independence, July 4, 1826. However, he did accept an invitation from Baltimore City a few weeks later to join in a procession honoring the memory of Thomas Jefferson and John Adams, both of whom had died on that date. On July 4, 1828, as the last living signer of the Declaration of Independence, he participated in a ceremony laying the first foundation stone for the Baltimore & Ohio Railroad. The gesture symbolized a life that began in the heyday of the tobacco planter gentry and ended at the dawn of democracy and industrialization. He died in 1832 at the age of ninety-five, having outlived both his son and his sons-in-law. His final action was one of utmost generosity. He bestowed his property on his daughters, Mary Carroll Caton and Catherine Carroll Harper, as well as on his granddaughters, with the stipulation that it be free from any control by their husbands. He thus ensured that none of his female descendants would be in the position of financial vulnerability that had characterized the lives of his wife, his mother, and his mother-in-law.

The house of Charles Carroll of Carrollton, overlooking Spa Creek, 1997.
Photo by M. E. Warren.

The Charles Carroll House

The house on Spa Creek remained in the family for another twenty years. In 1852 it was sold to the Redemptorist Fathers of the Catholic Church, who converted it into a nunnery. The frame house erected by Carroll's grandfather had suffered from neglect, and it was torn down about the same time. The nuns added another bay on the east side of the house and divided the top floor into bedrooms. In the 1870s the order built the present church and the rectory that connects the church with the house. The porch on the west side was added in the 1920s. It will be torn down when the house is renovated and refurnished.

Engraved by J.B. Forrest from a Drawing by J.B. Longacre after an original Portrait by Jarvis.

SAMUEL CHASE.

Samuel Chase

Maryland Historical Society

6

Samuel Chase, Politico

Americans who worked to establish a republic in 1776 had no ready models. They lived in a world of monarchies, kings and queens bolstered in their positions of power by aristocracies and legally established churches. The Dutch had set up a republic after obtaining their independence from Spain, but that experiment had succumbed to a monarchy in 1770. The Swiss had a centuries-old republican federation, but Americans knew nothing of its theoretical basis or practices.

As a result, republican theorists, both in Europe and America, had to look to ancient Greece and Rome for historical examples. And history was not encouraging. The republican city-states of Athens and Rome had been torn by strife, and both eventually submitted to military rulers who crowned themselves emperors. As a result, eighteenth-century political theory held that republics were inherently weak forms of government, vulnerable to self-interested factions. The corollary to this theorem was that a republic could survive only when led by men of "virtue," that is, disinterested patriots devoted to the "commonweal." The search for "men of virtue" to lead the nation is a leitmotif that runs through the speeches and writings of the Revolutionary generation.

To many in the Maryland political élite, Samuel Chase was just the opposite — he was a factious and divisive man devoted to a single-minded pursuit of his own interest. The image was not entirely accurate, for Chase was an ardent patriot with a gift for appealing to the interests and anxieties of the "middling sort" in the Maryland citizenry. He was a devoted husband and loving father who, despite chronic financial problems, was generous enough to take under his wing a covey of half-brothers and half-sisters, the fruit of his father's second marriage, who were the same age as his own children. He was capable of forming lifelong friendships with men such as William Paca, of impeccable social and moral credentials. Yet he was also given to rough manners and intemperate outbursts that offended many. His political philosophy always seemed to coincide with his own interests. He made mortal enemies, not only of the Dulanys and Carrolls of Maryland, but of some of the most prominent leaders of the early republic, including Thomas Jefferson, Alexander Hamilton, and James Madison. Samuel Chase, in short, was a complex man who almost defies understanding.

Chase's family background and baleful youth go a long way toward explaining his uncouth manners, unbridled temper, and single-minded pursuit of social status. His grandfather was a prosperous bricklayer of London, the owner of houses and land. His father, Thomas Chase, was college-educated and a priest of the Church of England. Shortly after being ordained in February 1739, Thomas sailed to Maryland to become rector of a parish in Somerset County on the Eastern Shore. He married Matilda Walker, whose father possessed a 240-acre plantation on the Wicomico River. On April 17, 1741, Matilda gave birth to a son, Samuel, and died in the process. Her father died three years later, leaving his plantation to another daughter and her husband. Thomas and Samuel Chase were on their own, entirely dependent on a parson's salary for support.

Thomas Chase, whose brother was also a Maryland minister and a friend of Lord Baltimore, somehow brought himself to the attention of the provincial authorities. The rector of St. Paul's Parish, Baltimore County, died in 1744, and Governor Bladen offered the position to Chase. The offer came, however, with an important condition —

Chase was to provide for the widow by furnishing her with 26,000 pounds of tobacco over the next two years. Chase accepted the offer, became rector of the parish, and rented lodgings with the widow for himself and his son. The parish included the recently founded village of Baltimore Town, whose explosive growth in the following decade would eventually make the rectory a lucrative position. For the moment, however, it paid only £100 a year, not enough to repay the debt to the widow. The widow sued him, and within two years Thomas Chase found himself in jail under execution for debt.

In the meantime, Thomas had made himself an enemy of the county sheriff by accusing him of cursing the king. Governor and Council investigated the charge, and the sheriff retaliated by accusing Chase in the *Maryland Gazette* of plotting to destroy him. Chase, emerging from debtor's prison after a year's incarceration, sued the widow for false imprisonment and the sheriff for libel. He won nominal damages against the widow and a judgment of £25 against the sheriff. Both by nature and by nurture Samuel Chase would inherit his father's aggressive pugnacity and his tendency to live beyond his means.

Samuel Chase's crude manners in adulthood suggest that his education in his father's household did not include training in the social graces, but otherwise his father gave him a proper gentleman's education in Latin, Greek, history, and literature. Though Samuel never attended college, he probably received the equivalent of what any colonial institution had to offer. In 1759 he left home to study law in Annapolis.

The standard method of legal training for persons of limited means in Maryland was apprenticeship in the office of a practicing attorney. The fee charged by the attorney ranged from £37 to £75 pounds sterling. In addition, the student was expected to pay his own room and board. Because of the rapid growth of Baltimore Town, and hence the congregation of St. Paul's Parish, Thomas Chase was probably able to afford these expenditures. However, his support for Samuel was meager, and the younger Chase was soon on the lookout for money-making opportunities.

The law office to which the lad of eighteen presented himself in 1759 was that of Hammond and Hall. John Hammond was a leader of the Country Party in the lower house of the Assembly and had little time for the legal novice. The education of Samuel Chase became the job of John Hall, a rising young attorney who would later play a key role in the politics of the Revolution. Although the two would ultimately come to differ politically, Chase retained a high respect for Hall throughout his life. Hall was not one of the colony's most expensive attorneys, and, perhaps for that reason, he was one of the busiest, handling about four hundred cases a year. Chase began by poring over the legal treatises in Hall's library and the records of past cases. Although Maryland, like most other colonies, did not begin publishing court decisions until after the Revolution, Hall apparently had an extensive collection of court reports, on which Chase took notes, arranging the legal principles in alphabetical order. He would reveal all his life a thorough grounding in both Maryland law and the English common law. By 1762 Chase was writing briefs, drawing up technical pleadings, and accompanying Hall on his rounds of the county courts.

Chase's social life, ever active, brought him into contact with two other legal trainees, John Brice III and William Paca. Brice, the son of a prominent Annapolis merchant, did not figure largely in the life of Chase or in the politics of the city. It is even unlikely that he practiced law with any consistency because he became preoccupied with spending his inheritance on the imposing mansion located at the corner of East and Prince George streets in Annapolis. Paca, on the other hand, became a close friend and political ally of Chase. Paca was the scion of a wealthy Harford County family and a graduate of the newly founded College of Philadelphia. Trained in the prestigious law office of Stephen Bordley, Paca had all the wealth, status, and family connections that Chase lacked. Paca, in turn, lacked Chase's dynamism, imagination, and rhetorical skills. In part because the two men complemented one another, they became lifelong friends and political allies.

With Paca's help Chase won admittance to the Forensic Club, one of several entertainment vehicles of the Annapolis gentry, combining witty discourses with music, theater, and wine. Chase became known for his course language and boisterous good humor, but within a year he was expelled for "irregular and indecent" conduct and unkind comments about fellow members. When not studying or carousing, Chase could be found courting one of the more reputedly beautiful of the Annapolis belles, Ann ("Nancy") Baldwin. The two were married on May 2, 1762. It was one of the few decisions in Chase's early life that was not founded on calculations of social and economic advancement. She brought neither wealth nor social status to the marriage. Her father, in fact, had recently died in a debtor's prison. It was a marriage of love, and children followed in rapid succession, but only four survived into adulthood: Matilda, born in February 1763, Ann ("Nancy"), born in 1771, Sammy in 1773, and Tommy in 1774.

Chase in the meantime had launched his legal career, winning admittance to the bar of several county courts in the course of 1763. At that point his father ceased any further financial assistance, remarried, and began raising a second family. He and his new wife produced three sons and two daughters in the next nine years. Thomas's wife died in 1772, and, at the age of sixty-nine, he undertook to raise the children himself.

Because of his youth, inexperience, and low social status, Chase's legal practice failed to attract wealthy clients or cases involving large sums of money. Like his mentor John Hall, Chase relied on volume to make a living. But, unlike other Annapolis attorneys, he devoted much of his practice to the defense of debtors. It was a clientele of potentially large numbers, but shunned by other lawyers because it lacked money to pay fees. Chase, however, found a certain kinship among such people, sharing their tastes and manners, and he may well have had a genuine sympathy for their problems. His caseload increased rapidly, from 170 cases in 1764 to 266 in the first three quarters of 1765. By then his annual income from fees was about £150 sterling, enough to support his growing family in modest comfort.

Chase's financial problems continued, however, for he had already begun to speculate in western lands. Land speculation was a common pastime among the Maryland gentry, but the more cautious ones, like Daniel Dulany and Dr. Charles Carroll, did so only after obtaining political influence, surplus capital, or both. Chase had neither. He speculated on credit, always a dangerous game. He began in 1762, nearly a year before he was admitted to the bar, buying proclamation warrants, wilderness lands which claimants had failed to survey and patent within the two-year limit allowed by the proprietor's land office. Because the holder of a proclamation warrant did not have to redeem the warrant until the land was surveyed and patented, Chase could build his estate while delaying a reckoning until his income rose. By 1764 he held 2,036 acres in his own right, plus a half-interest in an additional 5,446 acres held in partnership with another young attorney, Thomas Johnson. Once the warrants were actually paid for, Chase would be the landed grandee to which he had always aspired. Unfortunately. his modest income forced him to delay that reckoning year after year.

Chase's legal clientele, consisting of Annapolis artisans and small farmers of Anne Arundel and Frederick Counties, was a natural political constituency. Whether he realized this at the outset is uncertain; what we do know is that he launched a political career only two years after being admitted to the bar. In November 1764 Chase stood for one of Annapolis's seats in the House of Delegates of the General Assembly. Annapolis was still under the control of the proprietor's friends, as it had been in the days of Daniel Dulany. With the support of both the artisans of the city and of Charles Carroll, Barrister, leader of the Country Party, Chase took aim at one of the city's delegates, who happened to hold a proprietary office as well as a seat in the legislature. Under the banner "NO PLACEMEN," a Country Party slogan since the days of the Barrister's father, Dr. Charles Carroll, Chase won the election.

Although Annapolis was famed for its boisterous politics, it had never seen an election like this one. One Annapolis tradesman, Charles Willson Peale (soon to be sent to London for training as a portrait artist), wrote that "every engine was employed that each party could. The court dependents of office were threatened to be put out if they voted for Chase." On the other side, "banners were displayed to designate the freedom of tradesmen, and parades of this nature were made through all the streets with friends of Chase at the head of them." In Annapolis, as in Boston where Samuel Adams was mobilizing the "leather aprons," a new democratic politics was taking shape — even before the British Parliament enacted the first of the challenges that would ultimately lead to revolution.

Like his fellow populist in Virginia, Patrick Henry, Chase entered the Maryland Assembly just in time to play a role in the first of Britain's provocations, the Stamp Act. The act, as we have previously noted, was Parliament's first effort to levy internal taxes on the colonists (as opposed to import/export duties), and the Americans reacted violently. In August 1765, a Boston mob forced the Massachusetts stamp distributor to resign, and just a few days later a mob of Annapolis tradesmen paraded through the city (having gained practice in Chase's election) bearing an effigy of Maryland's stamp distributor. The frightened man fled to New York, and Governor Horatio Sharpe impounded the stamps on a British warship to prevent their destruction. With Chase in attendance, the Frederick County Court agreed to conduct business without stamped documents, and other county courts followed suit. In September 1765 a special session of the Assembly dispatched a delegation of Country Party leaders to a Stamp Act Congress in New York. In a December election John Hall won the other Annapolis seat in the lower house of the Assembly. By the end of his first year in politics Chase and his followers dominated the capital city's government, and he had gained a colony-wide reputation for resistance to British provocations.

Chase rose rapidly to a position of power in the Maryland Assembly, blending talents as a legislative workhorse, a skilled debater, and a mobilizer of middle-class voters. His law practice continued to prosper; by 1770 he was forced to skip Assembly meetings when the county courts were in session. He continued his land purchases, acquiring by the early 1770s an additional 3,500 acres both in his own right and in partnership with William Paca.

The Chase-Lloyd House on Maryland Avenue, circa 1885. *Maryland Historical Society.*

The Chase-Lloyd House as it appears today. *Photo by author.*

By 1769, Chase was convinced, in his own mind, that he had arrived among the Maryland gentry. William Paca and James Brice were undertaking fine brick mansions in Annapolis, and Chase decided to follow suit. For £100 sterling he purchased lot 107 (on the 1718/1743 plat map) at the corner of Northeast Street (Maryland Avenue) and King George Street. We know little of his house plan because he never finished it. It was basically a brick box with room for the future addition of wings. Chase brought over from England a man named Scott to supervise, and perhaps design, the work. And he retained an Annapolis merchant, Allen Quynn, paying him £30 for "overlooking" the project.

Construction began and expenses rapidly mounted. Chase sold to Paca his half interest in their joint speculation, disposed of another

1,040 acres to other buyers, and borrowed money. By the middle of 1771 construction costs on the house were nearing £3,000, and he had exhausted his resources. All he had to show for it was a basement, exterior walls, floors, and a well. At that juncture, one of the uppermost of the Maryland planter-élite, with more thought to his own interest than to the plight of Chase, stepped in as savior. Edward Lloyd IV, heir to a substantial percentage of the land in Talbot and Queen Anne's Counties, wanted a house in Annapolis worthy of his social standing. He purchased Chase's half-finished house for £504 sterling and £2,491 in current money of Maryland. Chase thus recovered his full investment in the house with a small profit, although the profit was zero if interest on the investment is taken into account. Even so, selling out was one of the better financial decisions of his early career.

When the Revolution broke out in 1775, Chase was in the forefront. He served in both the first and second Continental Congresses and on the Maryland Council of Safety, dividing his time among Annapolis, Philadelphia, and trouble spots across Maryland. His value to the patriot cause lay in his ability to appeal to the artisans and shopkeepers, the men who composed the "Sons of Liberty" and later the ranks of the Maryland Line, widely regarded as the best soldiers in Washington's army.

By the fall of 1775, Chase had concluded that the only solution to the imperial conflict was American independence, and in Congress he associated himself with the radicals led by John and Samuel Adams. John Adams found Chase "violent and boisterous" in congressional debates, but he liked the "ever social and talkative" Marylander. Chase's commitment to independence may well have helped sway Charles Carroll of Carrollton while the pair were on their Canadian mission in the spring of 1776. After his return from Canada, Chase raced to Annapolis to attend the Maryland convention that was considering independence. Finding the convention still faint-hearted, Chase went to the fountainhead of Maryland politics. On June 24 he wrote John Adams: "I have not been idle. I have appealed *in writing* to the people. County after County is instructing [its delegates to the Convention]. . . . Shall I send you my circular letter?" Four days later he wrote Adams triumphantly: "I am this Moment from the House . . . with an unan[imous] vote of our Convention for *Independence* . . . . See the glorious Effects of County Instructions — our people have fire if not smothered." Chase then returned to Philadelphia and happily signed the Declaration of Independence on August 2.

Despite his association with the "middling sort" in Maryland society, Chase was as conservative in his social and political views as Charles Carroll of Carrollton. He had no wish to see the existing social order disrupted, and he believed in government by a propertied élite responsible to a propertied electorate. His followers, for the most part, were men who could meet the colony's property qualification for voting; Chase had never sought the support of the rural landless or the urban poor. As a result, when the new state held an election for a constitutional convention in August, 1776, Chase broke with his former mentor, John Hall, who had joined Matthias and Rezin Hammond in calling for universal male suffrage. In the convention he worked with Charles Carroll and other Country Party leaders in drafting one of the new nation's most conservative constitutions. In fact, if Chase had won all of his hoped-for provisions, the Maryland constitution would have been even more undemocratic. He favored higher property qualifications on voting and officeholding, longer terms of office, fewer elected officials, and disabilities for persons who refused to take an oath of loyalty to the new regime.

Although Chase served in the Continental Congress until 1778 and helped draft the Articles of Confederation, the thrust of his energy in the decade after independence was in the Maryland House of Delegates. He was elected a delegate from Annapolis in 1777 — although only three voters appeared at the polls in his district, which suggested a certain disenchantment among the populace with the new Constitution. He would be the dominant figure in the lower house for the next decade. The Maryland Senate followed the custom of colonial upper houses in allowing legislation to originate in the lower houses, and thus the initiative lay with Chase, who arrived in the Assembly with an agenda of his own. When the second session of the new state legislature opened in June 1777, Senator Daniel of St. Thomas Jenifer wrote: "Yesterday S C opened his Budget of Business in a Committee of the whole House, and Carved out enough to take up the time of Six Months."

The first item on Chase's agenda was a legal tender act. Along with the other states, Maryland had financed its contribution to the war effort by issuing paper money. Since the state treasury had little or no gold with which to back the currency, it depreciated in value, as did the paper issued by the other states and the Continental Congress. In early 1777, Congress advised the states to make the paper currency legal tender in payment of debts so as to make it more acceptable. Chase agreed. However, the bill he drafted proposed to make it legal tender, not only for debts incurred during the war, but for the repayment of loans made in sterling prior to the war. This was the feature that stuck in the craw of Charles Carroll of Carrollton and his father. Not surprisingly, the measure was otherwise a popular one. It swept through the lower house on a voice vote, and Carroll was the only opponent in the Senate.

Although the younger Carroll accepted the act with resignation, his father, Charles Carroll of Annapolis, was outraged and wrote a series of nasty letters to Chase pointedly remarking on his lower-class origins and financial embarrassments. The letters stung Chase to the quick, and he soon refused further communication. Although both Carrolls suspected that Chase had drafted the act for his own benefit, Chase later maintained that he had suffered as much as anyone. In 1781 he claimed that he had received from his debtors more than twice as much as he had paid to his creditors under the law. "I have sunk by the tender law and the depreciation," he said, "two . . . well improved plantations worth £2,500 specie, some thousands of acres of land, and a sum of money in debts."

Although Chase and the younger Carroll determinedly refused to allow the tender law to disrupt their friendship and political alliance, the second item on Chase's 1777 agenda completed the break. This involved a pair of measures seeking reprisals against loyalists. The first involved a test oath to be administered to anyone suspected of disloyalty in order, as Chase put it, "to discover, if possible, our internal and secret enemies." The bill also imposed penalties for a variety of offenses, ranging from treason and sedition to discouraging enlistments and deliberately depreciating the currency. Carroll and other senators opposed the bill as a violation of freedom of speech and as contrary to the spirit of the Maryland declaration of rights. In the end the assembly compromised on a test oath to be administered only to officeholders and lawyers. Chase regarded Carroll's opposition to the test oath as making him "the advocate of the disaffected, tories, and refugees." He later recalled that Carroll's "Conduct on the Test Act created a Coolness, and a Suspension of our Former Intercourse." The two would remain political enemies ever after.

In the October 1777 session of the legislature Chase followed up the test act with a bill to confiscate the lands of the Baltimore proprietors and make all quitrents payable to the state. He argued that the measure would shore up the state's credit and help finance the war. To his dismay, John Hall offered an amendment to eliminate quitrents altogether, on grounds that they were an unfair tax on landowners. The house adopted the amendment, and Chase promptly resigned his seat. The house then rejected the confiscation act altogether.

Chase did not return to the Assembly until the middle of 1779. In the meantime, in April of that year, his father died, leaving an estate of seven slaves, some books, and household goods. The estate was left to Samuel for the care and upbringing of Thomas's four children, a responsibility that Chase readily accepted, even though his own wife, Nancy, had died some time earlier (the exact date of her death is not recorded). Nancy's maiden sister, Rebecca Baldwin ("Aunt Becky"), a longtime resident of the household, took over supervision of the children. Thomas's children, aged seven to fifteen, actually blended well with Chase's own brood of four, although it must have made for a noisy and rambunctious household in the structure that Chase rented on state circle.

With his finances stretched more thinly than ever, Chase undertook a series of speculative ventures, most of them involving wartime supplies needed by the state and the Congress. War profiteering had been a standard practice among merchants throughout the eighteenth century, although some were coming to regard it as unseemly in a fight for home and liberty. Chase, however, had no such compunction. Most of his dealings were technically legal, if shadowy, but one caused a universal condemnation that haunted him the rest of his life. This came to be known as the flour scandal.

In the summer of 1778 a serious flour shortage developed in New England as a result of the arrival of a French fleet and army. Congress ordered the shipment of 20,000 barrels of flour northward from the middle and southern states. In early August, Chase, still a member of Congress, advised the Baltimore City mercantile firm of John Dorsey and Company, of which Chase was a partner, to purchase large quantities of wheat and flour. When the Continental Army's commissary general arrived in Baltimore around the first of September to make military purchases, he found all the flour to be under private contract. He complained to Congress that its order to purchase, which should have been kept secret, had been leaked to Baltimore merchants. A congressional committee queried the Maryland delegation, and all but Chase denied being the source of the leak. Chase simply kept silent.

In October, Alexander Hamilton, a member of General Washington's staff, began a series of essays in a New York newspaper accusing Chase of having a "character as abandoned as any the history of past or present times can produce." With information obviously fed to him by the commissary general, Hamilton went on to expose the scandal and Chase's alleged role in it. Although Chase denounced the publication as a "false and malicious libel," his reputation was irretrievably damaged.

Chase's Annapolis constituency remained loyal, nevertheless, and in mid-1779 he returned to his seat in the House of Delegates. He immediately resumed his private war against the loyalists, introducing a bill to confiscate the property of all who professed to remain British subjects. Chase contended that the income from the confiscated property, when sold by the state, was needed to fund Maryland's contribution to the war. Carroll and others suspected an ulterior motive. Carroll noted that the property, if sold on short notice as it would have to be if used to fund the war, would be purchased at a fraction of its true value. The state would reap little; the real beneficiaries would be speculators. The lower house, obedient to Chase's leadership, approved the bill, but it died in the Senate.

Ironically, it was the action of Britain itself that revived the fortunes of the confiscation act. In 1766 the Maryland colony had purchased certain shares of stock in the Bank of England, to be used as backing for its paper currency. By the outbreak of the Revolution the stock was reputed to be worth £29,000 sterling. In 1779 the legislature asked its London trustees to sell the stock and remit the proceeds. When the trustees refused to do so the opposition to the confiscation act evaporated, and Chase's bill became law in 1781.

Whether or not Chase had proposed confiscation with his own benefit in mind, there is no doubt that, once the measure passed, he joined in the speculative mania that enveloped the state. Although nearly every patriot leader — except, notably, Charles Carroll of Carrollton — bought loyalist property, Chase was one of the largest purchasers. By 1785 he had obtained more than £6,000 of property in his own name, including the household goods and library of a member of the Dulany family. He also held a one-eighth share of the Baltimore firm of Charles Ridgely and Company, which, in collaboration with another company, had invested £55,000. Nearly all of these purchases were made on credit, leaving Chase with a debt that the income from his law practice, rising though it was, could not sustain.

Financial disaster was briefly postponed when, at the end of the war in 1783, the legislature sent Chase to London on a mission to recover the state's bank stock. His expenses were paid, and he was to receive a share of any monies that he recovered. He ran into a blank wall with the bank stock trustees (that issue was not resolved until twenty years later), but he had a fine time touring England, meeting government leaders, and making purchases for his family. Among the chattels he sent home was "One Chariott Complete," no doubt of a quality fit for a gentleman. A more enduring acquisition in England was a wife, Hannah Kitty Giles, daughter of an English physician. The bride was twenty-five (Chase was forty-three), of good education by eighteenth-century standards, and possessed a forceful personality. The Chase children, evidently accustomed to the light rein of Aunt Becky, resented her efforts at control, and there was tension in the Chase household until the offspring matured and married. After Chase's death Hannah Kitty and the progeny would engage in a bitter row over the estate.

Chase's financial collapse became ever more imminent when a postwar depression struck in 1784. The characteristics of the depression were a shortage of money and a collapse of tobacco prices. Hard currency was siphoned off to the mother country in payment of debts. The legislature aggravated the problem by authorizing the treasury to accept the wartime issues of paper money in payment of taxes. By the end of 1785 paper money in Maryland was almost as good as gold and nearly as scarce. The shortage of money combined with low prices for tobacco brought about a collapse in land prices. Chase and other speculators could get nothing for their lands, whatever their book value.

One solution — already experimented with in other states — was a new issue of paper money by the state, not for public finance (the sole purpose of all previous issues), but for debtor relief, in the expectation that the money would depreciate in value. Chase, whose politics never strayed far from his personal interest, liked the idea. In alliance with a debtor-friendly rural faction in the Assembly, led by Charles Ridgely (Chase's partner in speculation), Chase pushed a paper money act through the lower house in 1785. It was vetoed by the Carroll-dominated Senate.

In the course of the year 1786 Chase moved to Baltimore City. Annapolis, with its shallow harbor, had not been able to compete with Baltimore, and it never recovered the prosperity it had known before the war. Baltimore, on the other hand, was the boomtown of the Revolution, doubling its population in the course of the war and reaching 13,500 by the census of 1790. Writing to a friend, Chase expressed the conviction that he could "make much more Money by his profession in that place . . . and living as he does with so large a Family to support, it is absolutely necessary he should . . . get a great Deal." Sweetening the prospect was an offer from Colonel John Eager Howard, one of Baltimore's leading citizens, of the gift of ten city lots near the square laid out for public buildings. Howard's motive was far from philanthropic; he hoped that Chase, after becoming a resident of Baltimore, would use his political influence to move the capital there from Annapolis. He even offered an additional ten lots if Chase should succeed in moving the seat of government. Howard obviously knew his man. Chase accepted the offer and built a three-and-a-half-story brick townhouse on the site. Although he lost his Annapolis seat in the lower house, he was able to win election to the Assembly from Anne Arundel County. However, he never persuaded the Assembly to move the seat of government, and there is no record that he even tried.

When the Assembly opened in December 1786, Chase personally introduced a bill to print £350,000 in paper money. Newspapers promptly denounced the measure as a selfish scheme of speculators and large public debtors "intended to serve private, rather than public usefulness." Put on the defensive, Chase offered to bet his reputation against a farthing on the "propriety" of the measure. The Carroll ally who had taken Chase's Annapolis seat replied that it would be "an equal bet." The House of Delegates passed the bill by a narrow margin, and it was unanimously rejected by the Senate. That defeat, and the gradual return of prosperity in the spring of 1787, ended the paper-money war.

It also ended Chase's struggle for financial survival. In the spring of 1787 he petitioned the legislature "to be discharged from all his debts . . . upon surrendering up all his property for the use of his creditors." The Assembly, which, in response to the depression, had already passed a bankruptcy law, failed to act on the petition. It evidently felt that Chase could solve his problems under the provisions of that law and did not need special consideration.

By that date — that is, the spring of 1787 — Chase was embroiled in the final controversy of his legislative career, the attempt to form a stronger national union with a new constitution. A movement to strengthen the Articles of Confederation began almost as soon as the first attempt at national union had gone into effect in 1781. An amendment to the Articles that would have given Congress the power to levy taxes was sent to the states in 1781 and again in 1785. In the latter year it was linked to an amendment granting Congress the power to regulate interstate and foreign commerce. Each time the amendments failed to get the approval of all thirteen states, as required by the Articles of Confederation.

Samuel Chase agreed with the nationalist reformers that the Articles of Confederation needed strengthening. He supported the import tax amendment of 1781, and both he and the Assembly approved the commerce amendment in 1785. He was also involved in an interstate venture that would lead indirectly to a revision of the confederation, the Potomac Company. The idea for a joint venture that would build a canal around the Great Falls of the Potomac and clear its navigation west to Fort Cumberland originated with George Washington. In December 1784 he led a delegation of Virginians to Annapolis to secure Maryland's participation in the project. The legislature placed Chase on a committee to confer with the Virginians, and the result was the chartering of the Potomac Company in 1785. Chase bought a share of stock in the company for £100 sterling.

The Potomac project led to the idea of further cooperation between the two states on the navigation of both the Potomac and Chesapeake Bay. In 1785 the Virginia assembly proposed a meeting of commissioners in Alexandria and named a high-powered delegation that included George Mason, Edmund Randolph (soon to be governor), and James Madison. Maryland responded with a delegation of equal stature that included Chase. Through a miscommunication, the Virginia delegation failed to appear in Alexandria at the appointed time. The Marylanders sought out George Mason, who lived nearby. Mason, having learned of the conference for the first time, thought it a good idea, and located the Virginia delegate from Alexandria. Washington rescued the state's honor by inviting the group to Mount

Vernon. The conference signed a pact for the joint regulation of the river.

In the November 1785 session of the Maryland Assembly a committee chaired by Chase proposed broadening the area of cooperation to include military defense and a standardized rate of exchange for their state currencies. The committee further recommended that Pennsylvania and Delaware be included in the discussions. The Virginia Assembly replied with a proposal for a convention in Annapolis, to which all the states would be invited. Failing to see the dawning significance of these meetings that literally sidestepped the Articles of Confederation, the nationalists in the Maryland Assembly failed to name a delegation.

Delegates from five states convened anyway in Annapolis in September 1786 — Virginia, New York, Pennsylvania, Delaware, and New Jersey. The representative of New York, Alexander Hamilton, had come on his own initiative. At Hamilton's suggestion, the conference, which included Virginia's leading nationalist, James Madison, recommended yet another convention, to meet in Philadelphia the following May, to remedy "the important defects in the system." The proposed agenda was designedly vague, so as to alarm no one.

Chase, however, was beginning to have second thoughts about the direction of the movement for federal reform. The leaders of that movement had proven quite hostile to the sort of debtor relief measures he had been proposing for Maryland. Hamilton had close connections with private bankers in both New York and Philadelphia, and he was known to be a foe of state paper money. (Chase did not know that Hamilton was the author of the attacks against him during the flour scandal.) Madison had recently led the forces that rejected paper money in the Virginia Assembly. Whether these considerations motivated Chase we cannot be sure, for he never explained his refusal to attend the Philadelphia convention. We know only that when the Maryland Assembly placed him on the state's delegation, he turned it down.

Charles Carroll also declined to attend the convention, as did at least eight others who were nominated by the Assembly. As a result, the delegation that Maryland sent to the federal convention was decidedly mediocre. In addition, their attendance was so spotty that they had almost no impact on the proceedings. Luther Martin, a legal protégé of Chase, was placed on the delegation, but he fled Philadelphia in mid-summer when it became clear that the convention was drafting a blueprint for a strong federal government. He returned home to alert Chase and to draft a pamphlet condemning the Constitution.

When the federal convention ended and published its handiwork in September 1787, Chase instantly rejected it. The Constitution was certainly contrary to his interest because it expressly prohibited the states from interfering with the obligations of contracts (i.e., through debtor relief laws) or making anything other than gold and silver legal tender. However, he did not publicly base his opposition on that ground. Instead, he complained that the Constitution had created a government of virtually unlimited power, controlled by a distant élite, remote from people and inconsiderate of their interests. Even this sort of criticism was muted because Chase was standing for one of Baltimore City's seats in the Assembly in the fall of 1787, and the residents of Baltimore, artisans as well as merchants, were overwhelmingly in favor of the Constitution. As a result, the "antifederal" (proponents of the Constitution had begun referring to themselves as "Federalists") opposition in Maryland was led by Luther Martin and William Paca. Following the lead of Patrick Henry and Virginia's antifederalists, Paca focused on the demand for amendments that would protect the rights of citizens against federal tyranny. The argument was so attractive that James Madison promised in the Virginia ratifying convention that he would work for a bill of rights once the Constitution was approved.

When the Maryland Assembly met in November 1787, it immediately took up a bill to hold an election the following April for a convention to ratify the Constitution. Chase supported the call for a ratifying convention, having promised his constituents that he would do so, but he also gave a speech denouncing the Constitution. Federalists won the April election easily, for the Constitution was popular in all parts of the state. When the convention opened on April 21,

1788, the Federalist majority adopted a rule that debate would be limited to a discussion of the entire document, not a clause-by-clause analysis. They also agreed to keep silent themselves in order to hasten the final vote. As a result, Chase's sole appearance on the floor, in which he gave a lengthy diatribe against the Constitution, was greeted with "a profound silence," after which the convention adjourned for dinner. After giving Paca a day to draft some amendments, the convention on April 26 ratified the Constitution by a vote of sixty-three to eleven. Paca, having been promised that his amendments would be considered, voted for the Constitution. A committee then approved thirteen amendments aimed at protecting the rights of citizens, such as freedom of speech and press and the right to trial by jury.

Other states had proposed similar amendments, and when the First Congress assembled in May, 1789, James Madison, true to his word, introduced a series of amendments, ten of which, when finally ratified by the states in 1791, formed the Bill of Rights. The amendments answered most of the criticism of the Constitution, and antifederalism evaporated. Chase, however, did not wait for amendments to be adopted. As soon as the Congress approved a judiciary act setting up a federal court system in September 1789, he applied to President Washington for a position on the United States Supreme Court. Chase promised full support for the new government. Washington, who did not easily forgive political opponents, turned him down. Washington, however, did reward Paca with the position of United States judge for the District of Maryland.

The Baltimore electorate was equally unforgiving, and Chase lost his seat in the House of Delegates in September 1788. He never again held legislative office. Instead he obtained a succession of appointments on Maryland state courts over the next seven years. Gradually he worked himself out of debt. Aided by the bankruptcy act, he reached agreements with his creditors that allowed him to pay fractions of what he actually owed, and the Assembly obligingly canceled some of his purchases of confiscated British property. Gifts of land from the ever-loyal Paca helped to reestablish him as a landed gentleman, and by 1790 he was able to make some prudent investments in Baltimore City lots.

The French Revolution and the outbreak of war in Europe in 1793 completed Chase's transition to Federalism. The Washington administration's sympathies were with Britain in its struggle with the French republic, while the opposition, led by Jefferson and Madison (calling themselves "Republicans") sympathized with France. Chase, ever the social conservative, was horrified by the reign of terror that engulfed France in 1793–94. He came to view the Jeffersonians as subversive agents of French "Jacobinism" (a term that aroused as much apprehension among conservatives of the 1790s as "Bolshevism" would in the 1940s and 1950s).

Some of his dependents left home in the early 1790s. His eldest daughter, Matilda, married a Ridgely and soon presented Chase with a grandson. His sons Samuel Jr. and Thomas were in and out of the household as they attended St. John's College in Annapolis. A half-brother joined the army and died in the Ohio Valley Indian wars. Chase's grown daughter Ann remained at home, as did his half-sisters Ann and Elizabeth.

Chase's health began to deteriorate in the 1790s. He was afflicted by gout, a disease commonly associated with a lifetime of good eating and drinking. Chase had always been a large man, standing six feet tall, and his ample girth testified to his hearty appetites. It also made him a trial to fellow passengers whenever he took the stage.

Ill health, however, did not curb his style of living, and he soon found that the salary of a state judge was inadequate for his needs. Through friends he annually beseeched President Washington for a position in the federal government. Washington ignored him until near the end of his presidency when he began having trouble filling vacancies in his cabinet and the United States Supreme Court with able men. The salaries of federal officers voted by Congress were niggardly, and travel to the seat of government was an expensive, time-consuming burden. In 1795 Washington considered Chase for the post of attorney general but decided against him. Although he respected Chase as an able lawyer, Washington was concerned that he was "violently opposed in his own State, by a party, and . . . has been accused of some impurity in his conduct." However, the President changed his mind the following year and offered Chase a seat on the Supreme Court. Chase accepted, and the U. S. Senate confirmed the appointment, although several Federalists thought it did "not increase the respectability and dignity of the Judiciary."

The act of 1789 that set up the federal judiciary had provided for a Supreme Court of six justices. Below that were three circuit courts of appeals and thirteen district courts. While the district courts had justices of their own, the justices of the Supreme Court were expected to sit on the courts of appeals. "Riding circuit" over stump-ridden roads and unbridged rivers was onerous indeed, and Washington had trouble keeping the Supreme Court properly staffed. One of his Supreme Court justices had resigned to take a seat on a state supreme court, and another had resigned to become a state governor. By 1801, ten men had either resigned or refused an appointment to the Supreme Court.

To the surprise of many, Chase proved to be a highly competent justice and a net addition to the quality of the court. During the tenure of the first two chief justices, John Jay and Oliver Ellsworth, each member of the court issued his own opinion on a case, the outcome being determined by a majority. The opinions were delivered in reverse seniority, with the newest judge leading off. In his very first case, involving prewar debts owed to British creditors, Chase drafted a lengthy opinion so thorough in its research that his fellow justices had little to do but nod in concurrence.

Neither judicial status nor advancing age polished Chase's uncouth manners, however. The new justice had been immediately included in the social life of Philadelphia. Among the invitations extended was to be guest of honor at a dinner hosted by Pennsylvania Senator William Bingham. Mrs. Bingham had retained a French chef who produced a sumptuous banquet, complete with a variety of French wines. Chase surveyed the table and announced that he could find nothing fit to eat. Mrs. Bingham, ever the gentlewoman, asked what he would like and sent a servant out to find roast beef. The judge devoured this with great gusto, washing it down with beer. He then complimented his hostess for the "sensible" dinner, "but no thanks to your French cook." What Mrs. Bingham thought of this has mercifully gone unrecorded.

The late 1790s — the presidency of John Adams — was a time of intense party conflict, heightened by a diplomatic crisis that threatened war with France. Because there was as yet no tradition of judicial neutrality, federal judges unhesitatingly involved themselves in the fray. Chase, who regarded the Jeffersonian Republicans as inciters of mob violence and agents of France, became the most partisan of all. Though well-grounded in the law, he utterly lacked a judicial temperament.

The Federalist-sponsored Sedition Act of 1798 gave him the opportunity he sought to stamp out subversion. The law made it a crime, punishable by fines and imprisonment, to defame Congress or the president. Riding circuit and appearing in court alongside a district judge, Chase presided over the trials of several persons accused of treason or sedition. Typical of his procedure was the trial of John Fries, who had led a mob to free from jail certain persons who had refused to pay federal taxes. Fries was brought before Chase on a charge of treason. Chase opened the trial with a legal ruling, which defined treason broadly enough to include Fries's actions. Fries's counsel, who had been planning to argue that a vigilante attack on a jail did not amount to treason, was thus deprived of any defense. Fries was convicted and sentenced to death. President Adams, believing him to be misguided rather than dangerous, pardoned him.

Another famous trial involved James Thompson Callender, an Irish immigrant with a poison pen who had settled in Richmond. Several Virginians, including Jefferson, had slipped him money to encourage his anti-Adams tirades in the local newspapers. He was brought to trial for sedition and came before Justice Chase, then riding the southern circuit. The defense team included the state's attorney general and the son-in-law of Governor James Monroe. This quasi-official support for Callender was a red flag to Chase, who interrupted the attorneys' arguments and ruled the testimony of their witnesses inadmissible. The defense attorneys eventually sat down and refused to proceed, whereupon Callender was found guilty and sentenced to nine months in prison. In 1801 President Jefferson pardoned him.

The victory of the Republicans in the election of 1800 did nothing to soften Chase's partisan behavior. His fears for democracy and mob rule were confirmed in 1802 when the Republican-controlled Maryland legislature abolished property qualifications for voting and extended the ballot to all white men. His opportunity to speak out against the dangers he foresaw came when the circuit court met before a grand jury in Baltimore on May 2, 1803. Grand juries, informal bodies of citizens who investigated the potential for crime, had long been a vehicle for political harangues by Federalist judges. Chase's charge was literally a request that the grand jury investigate the government itself. "The change in the State Constitution," he declared, "by allowing *universal* suffrage, will, in my opinion, certainly and *rapidly* destroy all protection to property, and all security to personal Liberty; and our Republican Constitution will sink into a *Mobocracy*, the worst of all possible governments."

President Jefferson and other Republican leaders had come to fear the Federalist-dominated judiciary, especially after John Marshall, in the case of *Marbury v. Madison* (1803), invoked the doctrine of judicial review and asserted the superiority of the Supreme Court over both the executive and legislative branches. Casting about for ways to curb the Supreme Court, Jefferson's eye fell on Samuel Chase, clearly the court's most injudicious member. The president wrote to Maryland Congressman Joseph H. Nicholson, a member of the leadership in the U. S House of Representatives, suggesting that Chase's charge to the Baltimore grand jury might be grounds for impeachment.

Nicholson procrastinated, doubtful that Chase's harangue was grounds for removal from office. The Constitution provided for the impeachment and removal of appointed officials, including judges, but only for "high crimes and misdemeanors." Judges, on the other hand, were appointed for life during "good behavior." And therein lay the rub. What to do about an indiscreet judge, conceivably guilty of misbehavior, but who had not committed a crime? John Randolph of Roanoke, a Republican as impetuous and violently partisan as Chase, seized the reins from Nicholson's wavering hand, and on March 26, 1804, reported to the House of Representatives formal articles of impeachment. All of the charges against Chase related to the trials of Fries and Callender and the Baltimore grand jury charge. The House approved the articles; Chase would be tried before the United States Senate in the spring of 1805.

The trial was clearly a political affair, and prominent Federalists rushed to aid in the defense. The house members named to manage the prosecution were no match for Chase's lawyers, who brought in a parade of witnesses to testify that Chase's conduct during the sedition trials was exemplary. In closing, Chase's attorneys argued persuasively that the Senate would have to convict Chase of a crime, as required by the Constitution, in order to remove him from office. Although Republicans controlled the Senate by a margin of two to one, a majority of senators voted "not guilty" on five of the eight articles of impeachment. The remaining three failed for lack of a necessary two-thirds majority. Chase was saved, and so, in the long run, was the independence of the federal judiciary.

Except for his impeachment trial, Chase's role on the Supreme Court was a shadowy one after 1800. Chief Justice Marshall terminated the practice of *seriatim* opinions. Thereafter the Court would speak with a single voice, unless there were dissenting opinions, and most of the decisions were drafted by Marshall himself. Chase was also more subdued after his trial; there would be no more political harangues to grand juries. "My age, Infirmities, and the wicked Persecution I have suffered," he wrote a friend shortly after the trial ended, "have determined Me never to take any Part in any public Measure whatsoever." Declining health also limited his role on the court. He missed the court's entire term in 1806 and again in 1810. A young colleague appointed to the court by President Madison recalled later that Chase in his last years "could not be got to think or write." He died on June 19, 1811, and was buried in St. Paul's Cemetery in Baltimore. He played a prominent role in the founding of the American Republic; whether for good or ill is still a matter of debate.

William Paca, painted by Charles Willson Peale, 1772. His famous garden is in the background. *Maryland Historical Society.*

7

William and Mary Paca
and the House They Built

The year was 1763. Mary Chew had turned twenty-eight, and she was still unmarried. Most women would have had little chance of marriage at that age, and other prospects were even more bleak. Marriage was the only "career" open to women in the eighteenth century; they had no independent means of making a living. Even occupations such as school teaching, nursing, and clerical work were firmly in the hands of men. The disparaging label spinster reflected the fact that almost the only economic activity available to unmarried women was spinning thread from fibers "put out" to them by cloth manufacturers.

Mary Chew would escape such a fate in this year because she was no ordinary woman. She had two attributes that gave her uncommon independence — wealth and family connections. The wealth came into her hands through choice marriages by both her mother and her great-grandmother. Mary's great-grandmother, Henrietta Maria, had first married Richard Bennett, whose own father had been, for a short time, governor of Virginia. The senior Bennett had taken advantage of the executive's authority to make land grants, and engrossed huge chunks of the fast-growing Eastern Shore. He outlived his son and passed on to his grandson, the son of Richard and Henrietta Maria, vast tracts of land in Virginia and Maryland. Much of this imperial estate Mary would ultimately inherit.

Henrietta Maria's second husband was Colonel Philemon Lloyd, the son of an English merchant who had come to Virginia and acquired extensive tracts of land. Like the first Bennett, the first Lloyd was not a self-made man. He had brought capital from England and simply improved upon it in the New World. His son Philemon had moved to Maryland and owned a sizable fraction of Queen Anne's County, including the fertile island that formed the delta of the Wye River, known for a time as Lloyd's Island and later as Wye Island. This level tract of alluvial soil, some two and a half miles long and a mile wide, produced bumper crops of fine tobacco for more than a century, seemingly without exhaustion. The son of Philemon and Henrietta Maria, also named Philemon, married and had a daughter, Henrietta Maria Lloyd, who became Mary's mother. Mary's father was Samuel Chew, the fifth generation of that family in Maryland and Virginia, and possessor of several tobacco plantations in Anne Arundel County. Samuel died when Mary was only two years old, and her mother quickly remarried, choosing the most eligible widower in the province, Daniel Dulany. Mary thus grew up in the Annapolis household of the wealthiest man in Maryland, who increased his wealth by managing the estates of Henrietta Maria and her children.

Mary Chew clearly could afford to be selective in the choice of a mate, but caution was in order because the law gave a husband full control of his wife's estate. With her wealth, she did not lack for suitors. Indeed, one young man was so smitten by her that he replaced his own first name with her initials. When he signed his name "M.C.C. Homewood" to a legal document, it required a court decree to determine whether his signature was valid when written in this "very extraordinary manner."

Mary's quest ended in the spring of 1763 when she met a handsome young attorney, William Paca. His lineage was not as illustrious as Mary's, but it was respectable enough. His great-grandfather had arrived in Maryland about 1660, and his father farmed extensive tobacco lands in western Baltimore County. It is not certain where the first Paca originated. Though the name might appear to be Italian in origin, the pronunciation of it — with a long *a* — suggests an English origin. It may have been a corruption of an English name, such as Peake or Peaker (both of which were pronounced with a long *a* in the seventeenth century). William's father, John Paca, was a member of the Anglican vestry, a justice of the peace, and, in 1761, a delegate from Baltimore County in the lower house of the Assembly. William, born on October 31, 1740, was the third child of John and Elizabeth Paca and their second son.

Nothing is known of William Paca's boyhood, except that he was tutored in enough Latin and Greek to gain admittance in 1756 to the newly founded College of Philadelphia. Inspired by Philadelphia's foremost citizen, Benjamin Franklin, the college marked a new departure in American education. Older colleges — Harvard, Yale, even the College of William and Mary — were church-dominated and devoted primarily to the training of clergy. Franklin envisioned a secular institution aimed at the preparation of Philadelphia's sons for the world of business and political affairs. Instead of heavy doses of theology, the college's curriculum contained mathematics, modern English literature, readings in the philosophy of John Locke, Isaac Newton's *Principia*, and even an English translation of *The Four Books of Andrea Palladio's Architecture*. William's older brother did not attend college. Because he would inherit most of the family plantations, his "higher" education was in the tobacco fields. William, left landless, was destined for a professional career. He graduated from the college in 1759 and, at the age of nineteen, moved to Annapolis to take up the study of law.

His collegiate background and gentlemanly manners won him a place in the law offices of Stephen Bordley, the most successful attorney in the province. To be a clerk under Bordley was a coveted position, not only for Bordley's rigorous legal training but because he was able to give his young protégés the social connections so necessary in the colonial capital. Although Paca was not outgoing by nature, unlike his friend and fellow law student Samuel Chase, he was quick to make social contacts. Only a few weeks after his arrival in town Paca helped to form a debating society called the Forensic Club. Its membership consisted of fellow law students who were too young and too little known to obtain membership in the Tuesday Club, Annapolis's genteel literary society famed for its wine and wit. The Forensic Club met twice a month. The five-hour meeting included supper and drinks and formal debates on topics ranging from the relations between colony and mother country to the justice in the slaying of Julius Caesar.

After completing his studies with Bordley, Paca sailed to London in early 1761 to attend the Inns of Court. He remained in London only a few months, so the amount of law he absorbed must have been meager. Legal education at the Inns was perfunctory in any case; the purpose of the trip was simply to add to Paca's legal pedigree. In October 1761, shortly after he returned from England, Paca, Samuel Chase, and John Brice were admitted to the mayor's court in Annapolis. This was a court of small claims in which the main benefit to an attorney was experience at the bar, rather than any fees he might collect.

Although he earned small amounts of money occasionally handling legal transactions for Stephen Bordley, Paca by the spring of 1763 had yet to establish a law practice. Nevertheless, his widening social circle provided him the opportunity he sought. He met Mary Chew and quickly won her affection with his cultured manners, physical stature, and handsome visage. They were married on May 26, 1763. She was four years older than her husband.

It was a loving and happy marriage, so far as we can tell from the meager record of Paca's life, but her wealth cannot have been far from the mind of each partner. A house that properly reflected Paca's newfound status was the first priority. Only four days after the wedding he purchased two adjoining lots, one on Prince George Street and the other facing on King George Street. The price was a hefty £180, a sum that was almost certainly supplied by Mary.

There is no extant record of any kind of the building of the Paca house in Annapolis. The only hint of construction in progress came on September 1, 1765, when James Priggs, a laborer, stole from Paca 2,000 shingles and a hundred feet of wood planking, for which offense Priggs pleaded guilty before a court. The court ordered twenty lashes with a whip and ten minutes in the public pillory. The house may have been nearly complete by that time because on February 7, 1765, William and Mary sold a house and lot on School Street, where presumably they had been living. This suggests that their new home, or a portion of it, was complete enough for them to move in.

We do not know whether Paca himself participated in the design and building of the house. There is no record that he hired a designer or master builder, and several internal features of the house suggest the hand of an amateur. A few years later when James Brice, brother of Paca's lawyer friend, began construction of a mansion of his own on the corner of Prince George and East Streets, he designed it himself using English architectural handbooks. Paca may have done the same. As already noted, he was acquainted with the works of Palladio from college days, and he must have been struck by the grand townhouses of the English nobility in London.

The result, in any case, was a magnificent five-part structure of Palladian inspiration. The main part was a two-and-one-half-story block on a traditional plan of four rooms to a floor. Flanking the main block and completing the Palladian composition were identical one-and-one-half-story gabled wings, connected to the main house by recessed one-story halls, known architecturally as hyphens. One wing probably served as an office, the other as a kitchen. The house was built entirely of brick with carved wood trim, the roof of wooden fish-scale shingles. Five pedimented dormers in the roof afforded light for the uppermost half story. The brick of the main house was laid in a header bond, i.e., with only the ends of the bricks being exposed. The impression this conveyed was one of fine texture, high quality, and, of course, enormous expense. The walls of the wings were laid in English bond, alternating sides and headers. At the rear of the main house was a gabled tower that was probably used as a two-story porch over-looking the gardens.

The interior of the house contained a number of idiosyncrasies that almost certainly were the result of inexperience. The passageway between the front and rear doors is off-center, made so by the enlarge-ment of the parlor to the left of the front door. The asymmetry is emphasized by the placement of an arch halfway down the hallway,

Above: A mid-nineteenth century pencil sketch of the Paca House.
Opposite: The Paca garden as it appears today. *M. E. Warren Collection,
Historic Annapolis Foundation.*

which does not accord with either the front or the back door. The
staircase, instead of being situated in the middle of the entrance hall
was placed to the left, occupying an area that would normally be the
left-rear room of a four-room house plan. Instead of forming a spiral,
the stairway curiously turns back upon itself, so a person descending
encounters first a series of right turns, and then a series of left turns.
Calling attention to this rather bizarre result is the use of a turned
balustrade between the first and second floors and a Chinese-influ-
enced trellis between the second and third floors. Inconsistencies in the

The Paca House as a boarding house ca. 1890. A second story was added to the wings and hyphens in the 1880s to accommodate more roomers. Opposite: The Paca House as reception and registration center for Carvel Hall Hotel, 1901–1964. *M. E. Warren Collection, Historic Annapolis Foundation.*

detailing of the carved wood and plastering further suggest a lack of trained supervision.

The other three rooms on the first floor followed tradition, with a parlor and greeting hall on either side of the entrance hall in the front of the house, and a dining room at the rear. Apparently there was a porch-like sitting room on each floor of the rear tower

The gardens, which stretched from the rear of the house across the second lot to King George Street, probably took years to develop.

They were in place, however, by the early 1770s when Charles Willson Peale rendered a portrait of Paca. In the background are the gardens with a bridge across the narrow part of a fish-shaped pond. The Chinese trellis employed on the interior staircase reappears on the bridge. A small summer house, and a brick wall along King George Street framed the rear of the garden. Peale's depiction was of tremendous value when the gardens were restored in the 1960s.

In designing the garden Paca made use of mathematical principles available in most gardening handbooks of his day. By asserting these principles he sought to show the world that he was a man of refined taste and classical training. The idea was to create an optical illusion of distance (i.e., making the garden seem larger than it really was) by using principles that governed human eyesight. This was done by building a series of descending terraces, each narrower than the one above it. From the terrace at the level of the house, the garden path descends to a terrace sixty feet in width and from there to one forty-five feet in width. The effect was to create converging lines of sight that led the eye to the garden's focal point, the pavilion. As a result, the pavilion seemed much farther from the house — and the garden more spacious — than it really was. Paca and Charles Carroll of Carrollton may have been working from the same handbook, for the opposite effect — width, rather than distance — was created in the garden of the Carroll house.

The magnificent garden, as a setting for the house, was the subject of comment by every visitor. The Pacas' concept for a townhouse was by far the most ambitious yet seen in Annapolis, and it would be the model for a townhouse construction boom that spanned the next decade.

Because there is no record of construction, we do not know how much of Mary Paca's fortune the house consumed. However, James Brice kept a meticulous account of his own construction costs when he built a comparable house in the early 1770s. His house cost exactly £4,014 in Maryland currency (approximately $200,000 in today's dollars). This must have been about what the Pacas spent, for the two houses were given identical valuations in a tax assessment of 1798.

In addition to financing the house, Mary Paca may well have helped supervise its design and construction. William's law practice bounded forward in the months after his marriage, and it increasingly occupied his time. He qualified before the Anne Arundel County Court in June 1763, and within a year he had qualified to practice in the Frederick and Prince George's County courts, as well as the provincial court in Annapolis. Most of his cases dealt with disputes over debts and land titles, and his opponents were usually the men he knew from the Forensic Club, notably John Hall, Thomas Johnson, and Samuel Chase. Fast becoming a political ally of the mercurial Chase, Paca was active in the public meetings that protested the Stamp Act, and he helped Chase organize a county chapter of the Sons of Liberty. The public rewarded him for these efforts by electing him to the Annapolis Common Council in May 1766. The following year he was elected a delegate from Annapolis to the lower house of the Maryland Assembly. Such a schedule would have left little time for house building, and the day-to-day decision-making may have fallen to Mary.

Whether or not she was involved in the house building, Mary Paca had plenty of other responsibilities. In late 1764 or early 1765 she gave birth to a daughter, named after Mary's mother, but the child died in infancy. A son, John Philemon, born in 1771, survived into adulthood. Mary's mother, Henrietta Maria Lloyd Chew Dulany, died in November 1765, and her will added more property to Mary's already handsome estate. Mrs. Dulany also passed on to Mary the responsibility of a ten-year-old girl, the orphaned child of one of Mary's sisters. The child was afflicted with tuberculosis and died after only ten months in the Paca household. Befitting his enhanced status in Annapolis society, Paca arranged an elaborate funeral. He purchased more than eighty yards of white cloth, to be made into uniforms for the principal attendants, as well as twenty-one pairs of matched gloves. A custom-made casket, lined with white cloth, was built for the girl's corpse. The girl's estate paid the bill.

The Lloyd connection, so fortuitously achieved by Mary's great-grandmother, continued to shower its financial blessings on the Pacas. In 1770 Mary's brother, Philemon Lloyd Chew, died childless and left his entire estate to Mary and her sister Margaret. The most valuable part of the bequest was Wye Island, 2,795 acres of the most fertile land in Maryland. Margaret was married to John Beale Bordley, son of Paca's legal mentor. The Pacas and the Bordleys split the island down the middle, with the Pacas taking the eastern half. Bordley, of scientific bent, turned his half of the island into an experimental farm. He corresponded with agricultural reformers in England and put into practice the newest ideas on crop rotation, fertilizing, and deep plowing. Hoping to relieve Maryland's dependence on tobacco, he experimented with growing wheat, hemp, and flax. On the Pacas' half of the island was a tobacco plantation with ninety-two slaves. The successful attorney was now a landed grandee.

As Maryland rolled toward revolution, the political alliance between Paca and Chase became ever more firm. But the style and personalities of the two men could not have been more different. Chase was an orator and an activist who was happiest when haranguing a mob or leading a demonstration. Paca preferred the confines of his study and the service of his pen. As vestrymen of St. Anne's Church in Annapolis, both men became involved in a fee controversy of the early 1770s. While Charles Carroll of Carrollton and Daniel Dulany dueled in the pages of the *Maryland Gazette*, Paca entered the fray, taking on as an opponent the Reverend Jonathan Boucher, soon to become Maryland's most prominent loyalist. Boucher was, in some respects, an easy target because his own salary was affected by the governor's fee proclamation, but Paca's constitutional arguments, published in the *Maryland Gazette*, were favorably compared to those of Charles Carroll of Carrollton. After reviewing Paca's contributions to the debate one historian has judged him "the ablest constitutional lawyer of the province at the time." Annapolis annually reelected him to the lower house, and he represented the city in the convention of June 1774, the first in a series of conventions that marked the transition from colony to state. The convention placed him on the Maryland delegation to the First Continental Congress, which met in Philadelphia in September 1774.

In the meantime, Paca's personal life had been shattered. Mary died on January 15, 1774. She had recently given birth to a child —their third — and since there is no record of a lengthy illness, she may have died from complications of childbirth. The child, a boy given the name William, lived for only five years. The emotional impact on Paca can only be guessed. It would seem to have been severe, for he turned his back on Annapolis and all its memories. He moved his young family to Philadelphia and never again had a permanent residence in the Maryland capital.

Shortly after arriving in Philadelphia to attend the Congress, Paca formed a liaison with a mulatto woman named Levina. There is no record of her last name. She may have been his housekeeper, for, as a widower, he would have needed one. Although there is no record of a formal marriage, the relationship was not kept secret. A gossipy letter written a few years later by John Beale Bordley's second wife to her sister in Philadelphia described Levina as "very pretty," which suggests that she was seen in Philadelphia society. The couple had a daughter to whom they gave the name Hester, born on August 24, 1775.

Levina disappeared from the historical record thereafter, and within a year Paca was living out of wedlock with an Annapolis woman, Sarah Joice. In 1777 she gave birth to a daughter to whom Paca gave his own name, christening her Henrietta Maria. Sarah Joice came from a fairly well-to-do family, and by the time of her death in 1803 she owned a house and lot in Annapolis. Paca apparently took Henrietta Maria into his Philadelphia household, although when is not clear because by the time the girl was born Paca was married again.

In February 1777 he married Ann Harrison, daughter of a wealthy Philadelphia merchant. To his credit, he acknowledged paternity of his first natural daughter, Hester, and saw to her care, although it is not clear whether Hester lived with Paca and his other children or with the Harrison family. When the girl was five years old he entered her into a boarding school, the finest in Philadelphia and with the added advantage that it was in the vicinity of the Harrison home. In 1781 Paca wrote to Dr. Benjamin Rush, an acquaintance from their days in

Congress, to inform him that Hester, "a natural daughter of mine," had a frail constitution with frequent headaches and stomach upsets. He desired Rush to serve as physician should the girl need medical attention while in the boarding school. We hear no more of Hester, who probably did not survive into adulthood. She is not mentioned in Paca's will.

Not long after arriving in Philadelphia Paca put the Annapolis house up for sale. Built for Mary, it had no further meaning for him. The sale was not completed for several years, hardly surprising in view of the immense investment involved. In June 1778, a resident of Annapolis wrote to a schoolmate of Paca's that a "Mr. Wilson" had purchased the house for £4,500. The sale did not go through at this time, probably because the buyer could not raise the money. Paca finally sold it to fellow attorney Thomas Jenings on July 25, 1780. The price was £8,020, a sum that probably reflects the wartime inflation of Maryland currency rather than any profit that Paca realized. The sale ended any further connection with the "Paca House."

Paca was an active member of the Continental Congress, serving on a variety of committees and frequently called upon to draft resolutions and petitions. John Adams referred to him as a "deliberater," as opposed to his friend Chase, who was inclined to "speak warmly." But Adams appreciated Paca's "noble" sentiments on independence when the subject came before Congress in the summer of 1776. Benjamin Rush, who had exacting standards for every person he met, considered Paca "a good tempered worthy man, with a sound understanding which he was too indolent to exercise." Paca, like Chase, was well in advance of Maryland opinion on the subject of independence, and he eagerly signed the Declaration when the Maryland convention finally authorized it.

The war soon disrupted both the Congress and Paca's personal life. While Congress was completing the signing of the Declaration of Independence, the British army under command of Sir William Howe landed in New York. The British defeated Washington in battle and then chased him across New Jersey to the Delaware River. Congress, fearing that Philadelphia would soon fall into British hands, fled to Baltimore. The British stopped at Trenton, New Jersey, however, and went into winter quarters.

Paca stayed on in Philadelphia through the winter in order to woo and wed Ann Harrison. She was twenty and he was thirty-six when they married on February 28, 1777. Ann's father had died a decade earlier, and she had shared equally with her brothers and sisters in his large estate. She brought added wealth to the Paca household, notably in town lots and residential properties in the environs of Philadelphia. Despite Washington's capture of the British outpost at Trenton in December 1776, a British descent on Philadelphia in 1777 was all but inevitable. Paca accordingly moved his bride and his three children to the security of Wye Island shortly after the wedding.

Accustomed to the gaiety of Philadelphia, Ann Harrison Paca clearly regarded Wye Island as a social and cultural desert. She persuaded Paca to move the family back to Philadelphia that summer, despite the city's vulnerability, but the British once again interrupted their plans. In August 1777, Howe's army landed at the head of Chesapeake Bay. Convinced that an invasion of the Eastern Shore was imminent, Paca hastily organized the county militia. Howe drove his army north toward Philadelphia instead, but the British presence did encourage an uprising of loyalists. English evangelists sent to America by the newly founded Methodist Church had made a number of converts on the Eastern Shore, and these tended to be pro-British in sympathy. On September 6, Paca wrote to Governor Thomas Johnson:

> I am sorry to inform you of an Insurrection of Tories on the Borders of Queen Anne's and Caroline Counties headed by some scoundrel Methodist Preachers. A Body of eighty assembled in arms, were dispersed, three have since been apprehended [with the] Captain and Chief Methodist Preacher . . . among the Captives.

After defeating Washington at the Battle of the Brandywine, Howe occupied Philadelphia. The British remained in the city until the summer of 1778 when a new British general, Sir Henry Clinton, decided that he preferred New York for his headquarters. Congress returned to Philadelphia, and so did the Pacas, who moved in on the heels of the departing British, so eager was Ann to return to her family and friends. She made the move even though she was pregnant with their first child. On October 28 she gave birth to a son, who was given the name Henry in honor of her father.

The Pacas remained in Philadelphia for the next two years, although Paca himself spent much of his time in Maryland. He had been elected to the Maryland Senate in 1776 and was reelected in 1778. He attended every session until he resigned his seat in 1780. He also served for a time as a judge on the general court. He probably lived in the house on Prince George Street during these visits, for the house seems to have been kept fully furnished. Jenings sold his own furniture when he moved into the house in 1780. Paca no doubt came to wish that he had spent more time with his family because, before long, tragedy struck again.

In December 1779, Paca was attending a session of the Maryland Senate in Annapolis when he received word that his wife was seriously ill, and he promptly returned to Philadelphia. She had, in fact, been ill for some time and may never have recovered from the birth of her son. She died on February 25, 1780, at the age of twenty-three. Little Henry followed her to the grave in 1781 before reaching the age of three. Paca was left with his one child by Mary, John Philemon, ten, and his natural daughters, Hester, age five, and Henrietta Maria, age three. He decided to move his family back to Wye Island, and it was at this point that he put Hester in a Philadelphia boarding school. Whether his other children refused to accept her or whether he feared that the child might meet a hostile reception among his Eastern Shore neighbors we do not know. He maintained his residence at Wye Island for the rest of his life.

In November 1782, Paca was elected to the first of three successive one-year terms as governor of Maryland. The governorship was an office well-suited to his talents, for its duties were more honorary than onerous. The Maryland Constitution of 1776 conferred nearly all governmental power on the legislature and left the executive with little independent authority. The governor, in fact, was even chosen by the legislature. These were years of bitter infighting between Chase and Carroll in the assembly, and Paca was no doubt relieved to be able to hold himself aloof from that dogfight. The Revolutionary fighting had virtually ceased after the Battle of Yorktown in 1781, and preliminary articles of peace were signed in Paris at the very moment that Paca became governor.

His first ceremonial duty was to welcome Congress, which had decided to make Annapolis the temporary national capital in 1783. His second was to welcome General Washington, who journeyed to Annapolis in December 1783 for formal resignation of his commission. Paca delivered to Washington a flowery tribute that expanded at some length on the Virginian's virtues and deeds. Washington, with his customary restraint, merely replied that he was pleased to return to Annapolis "after the happy and honorable termination of the war." On Monday, December 22, a dinner was given at Mann's Tavern for over two hundred guests, and although there were the customary thirteen toasts, "not a soul got drunk," according to one observer. That evening Paca hosted a ball in the State House, which was brilliantly lit with candles in every window. Washington graciously made himself available so that "all the ladies might have the pleasure of dancing with him." The following morning Congress assembled in the capitol, and Washington tendered his commission with a one-sentence speech. One delegate found it a "spectacle inexpressibly solemn and affecting."

Demobilization of the army and a postwar depression caused considerable social and economic distress in 1783–84, but Paca could do little but beg the Assembly for proper action. He also begged the Assembly to authorize repairs of the drafty governor's mansion that lay just off Hanover Street (about where the John Paul Jones Chapel is today). None of Paca's entreaties met much response in a legislature convulsed by the conflict over paper money. Although considered an ally of Samuel Chase, Paca managed to avoid being dragged into that conflict as long as he remained governor. He maintained his interest in the law by conducting a seminar for young lawyers. A visitor to Annapolis in 1783 left this portrait of the governor's social and intellectual life:

Annapolis is a nursery of the long robe. . . . The Governor, who is of this profession, has instituted a society composed of students of the law, who meet at his house, at stated periods, to discuss law questions and questions in political economy. He proposes the subject, sits as President, and gives judgment, in conjunction with his council, the Chancellor, the lawyers and the Judges of the General Court. When debates are finished the company sup with the governor.

In 1786 Paca was elected to the lower house of the Assembly, and he promptly reestablished his old alliance with Samuel Chase. He voted in favor of an issue of state paper money that year, even though inflation was not in his own interest. He had joined Chase in various land investments, but, unlike Chase, he could afford to do so. Chase's continuing influence was also evident in Paca's response to the movement for federal reform. In early 1787, when the state was invited to participate in the Philadelphia convention that considered changes in the Articles of Confederation. Paca turned down the Assembly's nomination of him as a delegate, even though his idol, George Washington, had agreed to lend his own prestige to the meeting. Like Chase, Paca was no doubt suspicious of the creditor-minded people who were organizing the meeting, notably Alexander Hamilton and James Madison.

When the new Constitution was published in September 1787, Paca greeted it with strong objections. As Chase had feared, the document prohibited the states from issuing paper money, but Paca based his stand instead on the extraordinary powers given the federal government. He joined the call for amendments that would protect the rights of the states and the people. The trouble with amendments, as everyone realized, was that they opened up a Pandora's Box for change. Supporters of the Constitution opposed amendments, fearing that the entire effort at federal reform could come unraveled.

Paca was elected to the Maryland ratifying convention as an antifederalist, an opponent of the Constitution. In the convention, however, he and Chase faced a two-to-one Federalist majority. The Federalists made the rules, and Paca was not even allowed to introduce his proposed amendments. However, he was finally given assurances that he would be allowed to bring them forward after the ratification vote.

This gave him a face-saving way to break the Chase stranglehold, and Paca actually voted in favor of the Constitution. His amendments were then referred to a Federalist-dominated committee, which promptly buried most of them. In 1789, President Washington appointed Paca judge of the United States District Court for the District of Maryland. Washington initially had misgivings about the appointment because of Paca's opposition to the Constitution. However, when another nominee declined the office, Washington decided that Paca's contribution to the Revolution was more important than his aberration of 1787–88. Paca held the post for the rest of his life.

By 1790 Paca possessed more than a hundred slaves, and he was one of the largest landowners in Maryland. The Pennsylvania holdings he inherited from his second wife grew steadily in value as Philadelphia expanded after the Revolution. The farmhouse on Wye Island was inadequate for a man of such stature, so he decided to build a new house. This time he employed a professional architect, as well as a landscape designer to lay out the gardens and ornamental terraces. He again chose a Palladian plan with a rectangular two-and-one-half-story main house and wings joined to the house by hyphens. The ensemble was more than a hundred feet in width. The influence of the "Adamesque" vogue in Britain (called the "Federal Style" in America) could be seen in the roof balustrade, statuary on the cornices, and a large circular entryway supported by Corinthian columns. When completed, Wye Hall was surely the most magnificent private dwelling in America. To finance its construction Paca sold all of his Pennsylvania lands. The house unfortunately burned to the ground in 1879. It was still in the hands of Paca's descendants at the time, and it is likely that his private records and papers were consumed by the fire. The paucity of the written record of Paca's personal life has bedeviled historians ever since.

Paca spent his remaining years in the isolated splendor of Wye Hall. Except for his judicial duties, he had virtually no contact with people. His son John lived with him, but the two were never close. John was rumored to be something of a wastrel, although he married into the

Tilghman family after his father died and lived to the ripe age of sixty-nine. Paca saw very little of Henrietta Maria, who preferred to live on the western shore, probably with her mother. A tax list of 1798 indicates that Sarah Joice was a tenant on an Anne Arundel County plantation owned by Paca. Henrietta Maria married in 1794 and lived to be eighty-three. Paca referred to her as his "daughter" in his will and bequeathed to her a plantation in Anne Arundel County, possibly the one where her mother resided. In February 1799, Paca drew up a will for Sarah Joice by which she left her Annapolis property to Henrietta Maria.

The Joice will was Paca's last recorded action, for in the summer of 1799 he became seriously ill. He died on October 13 and was buried on the grounds of Wye Hall. He had been an ardent patriot who played a prominent role in the Revolution in Maryland. But, despite his service in the Continental Congress, he remained a man of local interests and provincial politics. He served his state well but had little grasp of his country's potential.

8

John Shaw, Cabinetmaker

Benjamin Franklin once informed an inquiring European acquaintance that America had a dearth of writers, poets, and portrait painters because its inhabitants were too busy rolling back the wilderness and creating farms and villages. They had no time for the finer arts. A Bostonian writing in 1719 echoed Franklin's thesis:

> The Plow-Man that raiseth Grain, is more serviceable to Mankind, than the Painter who draws only to please the Eye. The hungry Man would count fine Pictures but a mean Entertainment. The Carpenter who builds a good House to defend us from the Wind and Weather, is more serviceable than the curious Carver, who employs his Art to please his fancy. This condemns not Painting or Carving, but only shows, that what's more substantially serviceable to Mankind, is much preferable to what is less necessary.

Through the first century of English colonization in America rudimentary survival was the top priority for people living in a dangerous and pestilential wilderness. In such conditions, most houses and furnishings were handmade by the householder himself, with help from family and neighbors. Carpentry was squeezed in among other chores; there was no time for training or precision.

The appearance of skilled artisans, who could build great houses or piece together fine furniture, had to await the clustering of population into towns and cities, the growth of wealth, and the leisure to enjoy it.

As a result, there were no skilled craftsmen in America until the early decades of the eighteenth century and in the Chesapeake colonies, not until after 1750. Population and wealth created the market that allowed specialization, and that produced quality and refinement.

The tobacco grandees of tidewater Virginia and Maryland began importing household furnishings from England and, after their tobacco trade shifted toward Glasgow in mid-century, from Scotland. But they also welcomed the arrival of English and Scots craftsmen, especially those who could boast training in the mother country. Goods made by an imported tradesman carried almost the same signature of quality as imported goods themselves.

A truly fine cabinetmaker was more than a carpenter and a joiner. He had to possess imagination and the artistic talent to turn a vision into forms and shapes. He needed the patience of a perfectionist and a keen eye for detail. And, finally, he had to have some training in mathematics and physics to create pieces that bore large amounts of weight, yet seemed almost to float in space. John Shaw had all of these talents, and that is why his furniture is treasured even today.

Most artisans emigrated to the better known cities of Boston, New York, and Philadelphia, but John Shaw unaccountably landed in Annapolis in 1763. Perhaps he had a connection with the port through the Glasgow tobacco trade, or perhaps a Maryland-bound vessel was the best available. In any event, his timing could not have been better, for Annapolis was embarking upon a building boom that would make it the most glittering small town in America by the time of the Revolution.

John Shaw was born in Glasgow on April 25, 1745. Although little is known of his youth or training, he was almost certainly apprenticed to a carpenter or cabinetmaker. He sailed to America at the age of eighteen at a time when a major world war had recently come to an end. The war had left Britain dominant in North America and promised an era of peace and prosperity. Such a land surely had need of craftsmen, he may have felt. And so Annapolis did. Although the population numbered only about a thousand in 1763, it was the political, social, and cultural center of the colony. Wealthy lawyers and merchants had begun building magnificent townhouses there in the 1730s and 1740s: Charles Carroll on Spa Creek, Edmund Jennings (the present-day governor's mansion), Dr. William Stephenson (now the Ogle House). After 1763 even larger mansions were erected, as Maryland's *nouveau riches* competed for status: Dr. Upton Scott on Shipwright Street (1763–65), John Ridout on Duke of Gloucester Street (1765), William and Mary Paca on Prince George Street (1763–65), James Brice on East Street (1767–71), and Samuel Chase (1769–71) on Maryland Avenue.

Shaw probably joined the shop of a cabinetmaker or carpenter before venturing into business on his own. He first appears in the 1768 ledger of James Brice as a journeyman working on the Brice House. Brice paid him for labor and building materials relating to a variety of construction activities. He apparently began business as a cabinetmaker in 1770, for in that year the village silversmith engraved labels for him. He began advertising in the *Maryland Gazette* in 1771 and sold to James Brice two mahogany dining tables, a dozen chairs, and two card tables. The following year Shaw formed a partnership with a fellow Scot, Archibald Chisholm, an established cabinetmaker. The earliest piece of furniture bearing the Shaw and Chisholm label that survives today is a desk and bookcase in the Chippendale style.

Thomas Chippendale (d. 1779) was the most famous of English cabinetmakers. (The other well-known name, Heppelwhite, is more a genre than an individual, and its variations from the Chippendale are, to the novice, inconsequential.) Chippendale's ideas influenced the world of furniture-making through his work *The Gentleman and Cabinet Maker's Director*, first published in 1754, with a second edition in 1759 and a third in 1762. These books were widely used in America. There were twenty-nine copies among the carvers and joiners of Philadelphia alone before the Revolution. John Shaw almost certainly had a copy, whether brought over on the ship or purchased in America, because a number of his pieces follow quite closely the plates in Chippendale's book.

Chippendale was more an eclectic than an innovator. He borrowed heavily from the French (*Louis Quinze*) and blended their work skillfully with oriental and classical designs. Chippendale's trademark was solid construction that avoided the appearance of being heavy. He utilized the cabriole leg, which he borrowed from Holland, the claw-and-ball foot that originated in the orient, and the simple, uncompromising straight leg, sometimes tapered into a spade foot. His chairs, cabinets, and bookcases often featured fretted work, that is, slender strips of wood in a cross-work. The backs of his chairs, which were his most famous pieces, varied from gothic (the tracery of a church window), to curved ribbons of wood, to a solid piece set off by thin splats of wood. He was also especially successful in designing small tables with fretwork galleries for the display of china.

Chippendale had pioneered the use of mahogany, particularly as a decorative accent. Because mahogany trees grew in the West Indies, Americans had easier access to the wood and used it more extensively than the British. Although John Shaw's earliest extant piece of furniture was made in walnut, he used mahogany, or a blend of mahogany and tulip wood (also imported from the West Indies) thereafter. The interior and structural elements of his cabinets were usually made of yellow pine (known locally as "Anne Arundel pine"), and he sometimes used poplar for the walls and bottoms of drawers.

Shaw did not slavishly copy Chippendale. He imposed his own imprint on the style. Shaw's chairs and cabinets are generally more austere, less ornate than the Chippendale models, perhaps a reflection of the more primitive and puritanical American environment. His favorite chair or table leg, for instance, was a slender, square block, ending without a foot. Sometimes he tapered the square and set it on a spade foot the size of the original square (i.e. prior to the tapering). His later work, after the Revolution, was slightly more ornate. His table tops, for instance, in this later period, had serpentine shaping and chamfered (beveled) edges. The straight, square legs might have chamfered edges or even carved elements.

In 1773, the shop of Shaw and Chisholm announced the addition of

Joshua Collins, "a Musical Instrument-maker and Turner [i.e., lathe operator] from Manchester," England. By then the shop employed two journeymen and several apprentices. Their main contract that year was for work on the completion of the house that Edward Lloyd had purchased from Samuel Chase. They appeared in Lloyd's accounts as joiners, but they were also paid for various dry goods and foodstuffs for the house. Lloyd also seems to have arranged a contract for them with his Philadelphia brother-in-law, John Cadwalader, described by John Adams in 1774 as "a Gentleman of Large Fortune [with] a grand and elegant House and Furniture." The partners built for this new client a billiard table, perhaps one of the first in the colonies, for the game was relatively new in England. It was described in their accounts as a "Mahogany Missippy Table Cover'd with flannel & Green Cloth with a Sett of Ivory Balls for Ditto."

In 1775, Shaw and Chisholm received their first government commission to provide furnishings for the newly erected State House. They fabricated "a Pine Bookcase with 3 Drawers Pigeon Holes and Sliding Partitions" for the state's Loan Office. Like Patrick Creagh, Shaw depended extensively on government patronage in furthering his career. In November 1776, Shaw and Chisholm announced the dissolution of their partnership but promised that each would continue in the business of chair- and cabinet-making. Shaw would continue to work "at the house lately occupied by the company" at the foot of Church Street near the dock, and Chisholm would open a shop "at the house lately possessed by Mr. Charles [Willson] Peale, in Church Street." Peale had moved to Philadelphia to paint the political and military heroes of the Revolution.

Shaw was married to Elizabeth Wellstead Pratt on July 20, 1777. They would have five sons and two daughters, all but two of whom would still be alive upon Shaw's death. One son died in infancy, and the other four were educated at St. John's College. The eldest, John, studied medicine and became a surgeon at the medical college in Baltimore. He died while on a voyage to the West Indies in 1809. The second son, Thomas, opened a retail store on Church Street and prospered before moving to Frederick County. The younger sons, James

and George, worked for a time in the cabinet shop and elsewhere, apparently in anticipation of ultimately taking over the business.

A zealous supporter of the Revolution, Shaw was named state armorer in 1777, in charge of stocking arms and ammunition for the Maryland troops in the Continental Army. He purchased guns and gun barrels, probably fashioning or reworking the stocks himself, and in November 1778 he reported that he had 1,253 firearms and 1,093 bayonets in stock. He also joined the army in that year, receiving a commission as a second lieutenant, and served in the Maryland Line under General William Smallwood. The Maryland Line chiefly distinguished itself in the fighting in South Carolina in 1780, but by that time Shaw was apparently back in his civilian role as state armorer.

Opposite page:
The John Shaw House, circa
1896. *Maryland Historical
Society.*

The capitol dome suffered
several false starts and occa-
sioned the death of one carpenter who fell from the top.
John Shaw undertook the
final work and completed it in
1794. He placed the acorn on
the pinnacle as a symbol of
wisdom. *Photo by author*

The John Shaw House on
State Circle. The balcony was
added by a later owner.
Photo by author.

The Council paid for the use of his tools and workmen in the manufacture of cartridge boxes and packing cases for guns, as well as for mending windows and putting up shelves in the armory itself. He would retain the post of state armorer until 1819. He also made camp furniture for the army, as well as bedsteads and coffins. Indeed, by the end of the war he had a thriving funeral business, both civilian and military.

By 1783, Shaw's shop near the dock on Church Street had branched out into a number of retail lines. He sold imported furniture and large quantities of sailcloth. He regularly exchanged goods with other merchants located on the dock, notably John Randall and John Davidson. Shaw regularly bought the hardware for his furniture from Davidson, for instance, and he supplied the two retail merchants with lumber. A tax list of 1783 indicates that the wealth of the artisans Shaw and Chisholm was about equal to that of the retail merchants Randall and Davidson. The tax list also indicated that Shaw and Chisholm were the only cabinetmakers in the town at that time. There had been six such artisans in 1775. These may have moved to Baltimore Town, which quickly surpassed Annapolis as the commercial center of Maryland after the Revolution.

When George Washington came to Annapolis in December 1783 to resign his commission from the army, Shaw was put in charge of preparing the State House for the festivities. The state reimbursed him for the purchase of planks and nails for the platform, glazing for the windows, and candles to illuminate the banquet and dance floor.

In early 1783, a fire destroyed Shaw's place of business, causing the loss of all his tools and "every other thing in his shop." For a brief time he reestablished his partnership with Chisholm, and an advertisement in a November 1784 edition of the *Maryland Gazette* proclaimed that their stock had been enlarged to include "maps of North America, divided according to the preliminary articles, signed at Versailles [and a] General Atlas describing the whole universe." Shaw and Chisholm each continued in the retail trade until the end of the century.

In 1784 Shaw purchased a house on the west side of state circle facing the State House. Built in the 1720s, it was of one-and-a-half stories with gambrel roof, similar to the Patrick Creagh house built about the same time. Because of the slope of state circle, the basement was open on one side, and Shaw no doubt used it for his cabinet-making and retail operations. Its proximity to the State House also made it convenient for Shaw to carry out his various government commissions, as well as in generating new business. The move of the Continental Congress into the Maryland State House improved his custom. Shaw sold cabinet work in the amount of £4.2.6 to Thomas Jefferson. Charles Willson Peale, who completed another portrait of Washington that year (his third), wrote to Governor Paca from Philadelphia to suggest that Shaw and Chisholm be employed to unwrap and hang the heavily framed piece in "a public Building."

Shaw's business with the government was steady and profitable. In 1785 he produced two tables and a cupboard for the House of Delegates, and the following year the legislature purchased two pine tables for its committee rooms and a number of mahogany rulers. In 1791 the Council directed Shaw "to make such repairs in the windows and fire places in the House of Delegates as are necessary, and to procure tables, benches, curtains to two windows, coverings for the tables, and one and a half doz tin sconces, and to take the same into his possession at the end of the Session." In 1792, Shaw won a bid to serve as general contractor for the completion of the State House, including the dome. He supervised the work of carpenters and plasterers as subcontractors. Specifications in Shaw's handwriting that survive indicate a fair grounding in the fundamentals of architecture and structural engineering.

As the state prospered toward the end of the century, the tastes of legislators grew more luxuriant. In 1794 Shaw replaced the covering on the senators' chairs and installed a crimson curtain on the president's desk. In the House of Delegates he recovered the speaker's chair with "Crimson moreen [a fabric having a moiré, or watered, finish] & Brass nails" and installed a curtain on his desk. In May 1796, Shaw was commissioned "to make for the use of the Executive in the Council Room Six arm Chairs of Mohogany with stuffed bottoms covered with crimson Moriens." In December of that year the government ordered "twenty four handsome commodious chairs to be made for the accommodation of the Senate among which shall be a presidential chair." With less frequency Shaw supplied tables, chairs, and bookcases to the State House for the next twenty years.

The partnership with Archibald Chisholm had been dissolved in late 1784, and the succeeding decade and a half was the most productive — and imaginative — of Shaw's artistic career. He and Chisholm continued to dominate the trade in Annapolis, with occasional competition from former students, such as Joseph Middleton. Their modifications of the Chippendale style — incorporating by the 1790s the Heppelwhite influence from England — has been treated by students of furnishings as an "Annapolis style."

Characteristic of this style was a circular card table, to which Shaw affixed his label in 1796. Probably adapted from plates in George Heppelwhite's *Cabinet-Maker's and Upholster's Guide* (published in 1788 with a second edition in 1794), the round table was hinged in the middle for easy storage. Its frame was of yellow pine with mahogany veneer and oak hinges. The straight, tapered legs ended in ovate spade feet cut from a solid block. A pilaster at the top of each leg contained a carved eagle with star banner and American shield enclosed in an oval. This touch — uncharacteristic of Shaw — may have been demanded by the person for whom the table was made, or it may have reflected the influence of a "Federal style" being developed by the craftsmen of Baltimore. In general, Shaw adhered during these years to a stylistic format — unadorned silhouette, little or no carved ornamentation (woodcarving was not his forte), repeated mouldings, particularly on the edges of table tops, and the restrained use of inlays.

Another example from this period is a sideboard that Shaw made to the order of Robert Goldsborough. Its functional section was of five parts, each equal in size. At each end were drawers with interior racks for liquor bottles. The three middle compartments were cupboards with hinged doors. The cupboard doors received a rich, yet restrained decorative treatment consisting of cross-banded strips of mohogany veneers, which give a rippling effect. Although the piece looks heavy, it seems to float on tapered legs terminating in rounded spade feet. The sideboard probably sat in a windowed bay of the dining room of the Goldsborough home, Myrtle Grove, opposite a painting of the Goldsborough family by Charles Willson Peale.

If the specimens that survive today reflect the stock available in Shaw's inventory in the 1790s, he specialized in sideboards, side chairs, breakfast or Pembroke tables, card tables, chests of drawers, desks, and bookcases. Easy chairs and sofas, bedsteads, and chests of drawers he made, but apparently not in abundance.

John Shaw's method of doing business changed by 1800, paralleling changes that were occurring in the workshops of craftsmen in Philadelphia, New York, and Boston. The change was wrought by a growing demand for American-made furniture among the urban middle class. Traditionally, in both England and America, the master craftsman had worked side by side with his employees, journeymen and apprentices, supervising their work, and contributing his own knowledge and skills. The craftsman's shop in the eighteenth century was a convivial place in which there were neither class lines nor firm distinctions between employer and employee. Liquor was commonly one of the bonds that held the relationship together, as the entire shop might adjourn two or three times a day to a nearby tavern.

By 1800 this cozy fraternal style was beginning to fall apart. The master craftsman, like Shaw, had become a businessman, responsible not only for the sale of the merchandise but the stocking of lumber, inlays, veneers, stains, varnishes, and hardware. Storage of his materials often required the purchase of additional land and buildings. His capital investment, or interest on borrowed capital, became as important a consideration as his employees' wages, and together they occupied nearly all his time. Rarely, then, by the end of the eighteenth century, did the master craftsmen actually work on a piece of furniture, unless it be a piece specially ordered that carried a goodly price tag. Yet, because the pieces that left his shop carried his label, the master had to be conscious of upholding quality. He was no longer a worker, however; he was instead a capitalist, an employer, boss, and supervisor.

With this changing role of the master craftsman came a subtle change in the social order within the shop. A gap had opened between employer and employees. The social hour in the neighborhood tavern became a distant memory as the master carefully counted working hours and paid wages accordingly. Eventually the division between capital and labor produced friction, and, after 1815, even strikes by workingmen, though there is no evidence of labor trouble in the shop of John Shaw.

The great benefit of the growing divide between capital and labor was that it led to a division of labor and more efficient methods of production. Employees could be trained to specialize in certain tasks — the turning of chair arms and legs, applying of veneer, padding and upholstering sofas and easy chairs. The product was more uniform and displayed less ingenuity, but it was far less expensive to produce. An example of this method of production is a sofa produced by Shaw's shop, probably around 1790. With eight tapered straight legs, joined by stretchers and welcoming arms curving onto arm rests, the piece is basically in the Chippendale style. Yet there is nothing to distinguish it from sofas being made at this time by other cabinetmakers from Baltimore to Boston. Significantly, it is the only sofa made in Shaw's shop after 1790 (among those that survive today) that displays his label. Perhaps he regarded the genre not distinctive enough to be worth claiming authorship.

The other result of this new method of furniture-making (carried to the verge of mass production by Duncan Phyfe in New York) was that it tended to freeze Shaw's style of design. After 1800 styles of furniture in the Atlantic world changed dramatically through the influence of the ideas of Thomas Sheraton in England and the development of the "Imperial Style" in Napoleonic France. If Shaw was aware of these changes, he made no effort to adapt to them. He even ignored the American "Federal Style" developed in Baltimore and cities to the north. In the 1820s he was still producing his own austere version of the Chippendale.

Elizabeth Pratt Shaw died in 1793, and although Shaw married again five years later, his elder daughter, Mary, remained unmarried and lived with him the rest of his life. In 1798 Shaw married Margaret Steuart, of whom little is known except the near certainty of her Scottish ancestry. They had one daughter, Jane, who did not survive to adulthood. Margaret herself died in 1806.

Besides his business interests, Shaw's time was occupied after 1800 with the public service expected of a successful resident of the community. He served on the Annapolis city council from 1801 to 1812 and was elected to the legislature in 1806. Throughout these years he was a member of the vestry of St. Anne's Church. In 1818 his younger daughter Elizabeth married Thomas Franklin, a well-to-do shopkeeper.

Shaw died on February 26, 1829, at the age of eighty-four. By his will he left to his son George the house and shop on state circle, plus "the Store House he now occupies," with the proviso that George pay a "reasonable rent" on these properties to Shaw's other descendants. To his youngest son James, Shaw conveyed a lot and buildings lying on Doctor's Street in Annapolis. The absence of any conveyance of property, other than servants, to his older sons, John and Thomas, suggests that they may have become independently wealthy. The remainder of his real estate in Annapolis and "elsewhere" he gave in common to all his children and their spouses. Each daughter received a slave woman together with her daughter, and each son received a male slave. All of Shaw's personal possessions went to the family in common, presumably to be divided among themselves.

George Shaw died only two months after his father did, and the family business passed to Elizabeth's husband Thomas Franklin. Whether he was able to carry it on seems doubtful, for by then furniture- and cabinet-making had almost ceased to be an art. The craftsman of the eighteenth century had yielded to the unskilled machine operator, and the casual, indulgent workplace had been replaced by the cheerless, impersonal factory.

JONAS GREENE, PRINTER OF MARYLAND GAZETTE. 1745.

Anne Catherine Green (1720-1775) painting by Charles Willson Peale, 1769. *National Portrait Gallery, Smithsonian Institution*

Jonas Green, printer of *Maryland Gazette*, 1745. *Maryland Historical Society*

9

Jonas and Catherine Green: The Journalist as Revolutionary

The American Revolution was unique among the great revolutions of modern times. It was a revolution without ideology and, at least in the beginning, without a common goal. The agitators of the 1760s — Samuel Adams in Massachusetts, Samuel Chase in Maryland, Patrick Henry in Virginia — were not working *for* something. They knew only what they were against — acts of Parliament that affected the internal affairs of the colonies. In this sense they were the successors to decades of Country Party agitation against the use and abuse of power by colonial governors. The transition from "country" opposition to active nation building, however, was slow and ponderous. Not until fighting actually broke out in 1775 did a majority of Americans actively consider the possibility of outright independence.

At that point Samuel Adams boasted that he had favored independence ever since 1768. If so, there is nothing in his public statements or private papers to indicate it. To advocate independence publicly prior to 1775 would have been dangerous indeed, for such a stand was tantamount to treason. The English treason act was not a pretty thing to read, and its history was uglier still: a story of pain and brutality as a weak government in London, lacking a standing army or even a civilian police force, sought to keep an unruly populace under control by meting out stiff punishments to those who dared rebel.

Given this tradition, of which every colonist was aware, no American leader could publicly commit to independence without substantial assurance of public support.

In the evolution of public opinion from 1765 to 1775 no institution played a greater role than the colonial newspaper. Although the newspaper was a fairly recent development (the first one in America was founded in Boston in 1709), it had become an important vehicle for reflecting as well as in shaping popular thought. Every colonial city had one or more, and they were invariably Whiggish and anti-imperial. There was no journalistic spokesman for the loyalist cause until after the Revolution broke out. Although the papers were small, consisting usually of four pages on a single folded sheet of paper, poorly printed, and relatively expensive, their weekly appearance was eagerly awaited. The news in them might be from three to eight weeks old, due to the slowness of the post and dissemination by travelers, but it was fresh to its readers. There was as yet no concept of an editorial, but contributions from readers, usually protected by pseudonyms, carried forth the public debate. Each edition was small in numbers, due to the primitive condition of the printer's art, but the sheets were eagerly passed from hand to hand, nailed to the walls of taverns, and sent in batches to relatives in the countryside. Newspapers were crucial to the creation of the American Republic.

Among the most important of the journalistic torchbearers of the Revolution were Jonas and Catherine Green. Their vehicle was the *Maryland Gazette* of Annapolis.

Jonas Green's pedigree boasted three generations of printers in America. His great-grandfather, Samuel Green, was part of the Puritan exodus that founded the Massachusetts Bay Colony in 1630. The first printing press in America was set up at Harvard College, and when its operator died, Samuel Green became official printer to the college and the colony. Samuel was the father of nineteen children, of whom three sons learned the printing craft under his tutelage. The eldest of these, Samuel Jr., had a son whom he named Timothy and also trained to be a printer. Jonas Green, born in 1712, was the fifth son of Timothy

Green and Mary Flint of Boston. The year after Jonas was born his family moved to New London, Connecticut, where Timothy became printer to the governor and company of that colony.

Following family tradition, Jonas was apprenticed to a printing shop in Boston to learn the craft. He and his brother then worked as journeymen printers for the firm of Kneeland & Green in Boston. In the mid-1730s, Jonas moved to Philadelphia and found employment in the shop of Benjamin Franklin, who had purchased a press in 1728 and had already established a newspaper and an annual almanac. On April 25, 1738, Green married, in Christ Church, Philadelphia, Anne Catherine Hoof, who had been brought to America from Holland in her early childhood. Over the next two decades the couple would have six sons and eight daughters. Of the fourteen, only six survived childhood. The three surviving sons all continued the family's typographical tradition.

In 1738, Maryland's Governor Samuel Ogle paid a visit to Philadelphia and somehow communicated the word that Maryland was in need of a new official printer. The previous printer, William Parks, had run afoul of the government because his newspaper (the first to appear in Maryland), the *Maryland Gazette*, had been too closely associated with the Country Party. Parks shut down his paper in 1734 and moved to Williamsburg where he founded the *Virginia Gazette*. The opening in Maryland was just the sort of news for which Benjamin Franklin had a particularly keen nose, and, no doubt with his blessing, Green applied for and got the job. Jonas and Anne Catherine moved almost immediately to Annapolis, for their first-born child was baptized in Saint Anne's Church in October 1738.

The Greens moved into a fine brick-and-frame house on Charles Street. It was one of the oldest in the city, having been built shortly after the turn of the century, and it remains one of the two oldest in the city today. The printing shop was probably housed in a small brick building behind the house. That the printing business was separate from the living quarters is evident from the notice that Green inserted in his newspaper on January 20, 1757:

Eighteenth-century colonial printer's shop.
Opposite, above: The house of Jonas and Anne Catherine Green on Charles Street as it appears today. The present owner is a direct descendent of the Greens. *Photo by author.*
Opposite, below: The Green House, ca. 1900. *Historic Annapolis Foundation Collection.*

Many of my Customers, during the Time of the Small-Pox was lately in my Family, which was about seven Weeks, it seems were afraid to receive their GAZETTE, lest they should convey the Infection; but their Fears were Groundless (even if it could be convey'd by Paper), for the Press and Paper were always kept at a good Distance from the Rooms where that Distemper was: However, to remove all Doubts and Fears about it, I can now acquaint them, that my House is quite clear of the Small-Pox, and no person in it liable to it; nor in any one Family in the Street where I live.

J. GREEN

The printer's shop in the eighteenth century was an untidy, ink-stained, crowded place to work. The centerpiece of it was the wooden press, usually purchased secondhand and brought from England. It

175

had not evolved much from the crude contraption put together by Johann Gutenberg two hundred years earlier. Type, laid by hand one letter at a time and inked with a leather ball, was engraved upon paper by pressing together two wooden plates, using a large wooden screw. Each sheet of paper required a separate operation. The master printer set the type and operated the press; an apprentice smeared the ink and replaced the paper. The process was so laborious that a book might take a year to produce; newspaper circulation was limited to a few hundred copies.

Further complicating the printing process was the scarcity of type. Prior to 1772, when a type foundry was imported from Germany and established at Germantown, Pennsylvania, printer's type had to be imported from Europe. It was accordingly expensive, and most printers could afford to keep on hand only a few forms of each letter or punctuation mark. This explains in part the preference for newspapers over books (most of which were imported from England) in the American colonies. Printers preferred a periodical literature where they could set type, print, and then scramble the type for the next job.

The best paper and ink were also imported, although inferior forms of each were made in the colonies. Paper factories were few and there were none in Maryland. Jonas Green had to buy his paper in Philadelphia. When European supplies of ink were interrupted by warfare in the 1740s, Green purchased ink in Philadelphia or made his own out of lampblack and linseed oil.

Since he was employed as the public printer, it is scarcely surprising that Green's first publication in Annapolis was the *Votes and Proceedings* of the Assembly and a *Collection of the Governor's Several Speeches* of the year 1739. There was a steady if modest income from such public jobs, but it was not enough to ensure prosperity. As a result, Green before long was giving thought to the establishment of a newspaper. It was a sideline common enough among American printers, including Green's mentor, Benjamin Franklin. But it imposed new responsibilities, for the printer also had to function as editor, publisher, and occasionally as a reporter.

Green resurrected the name abandoned by William Parks eleven years earlier and launched the *Maryland Gazette*, a weekly paper, in April 1745. It was an instant success. Two years later Green wrote to Franklin that he had "about 450 or 460 good Customers for Seal'd Papers, and about 80 unseal'd." He was using three or four reams of paper a week and was in constant want of more. He promised Franklin that he would send a bill of £45 sterling if Franklin would procure some paper and four or five pounds of lampblack. However, Green also confessed that he had some difficulty collecting from his subscribers and that the Assembly had prohibited him from resorting to the law courts. Though newspapers in the eighteenth century did carry advertisements, publishers derived most of their income from their subscription lists. Consequently, Green was much dependent on the £260 in Maryland currency that he received for his "Public Work," and he assured Franklin that he would send "a good Bill" when he was next paid by the Assembly.

As a printer, Jonas Green was a mere tradesman. As a newspaper editor and publisher, he was a man of social and political importance. His growing stature in the community was evident when, on August 2, 1748, he was initiated into the Tuesday Club, founded three years earlier by Dr. Alexander Hamilton, a Scottish physician who had landed in Maryland in 1739. Finding Annapolis society both tedious and provincial, Hamilton sought to enliven it by forming a club organized on the lines of one he had known in his native Edinburgh and which he remembered fondly for its convivial evenings of conversation and drinking. In May 1745 he brought together eight men, four of them Scots, who resolved to meet every Tuesday (they soon changed it to every other Tuesday) for conversation, music, and ribald humor. To prevent the heavy drinking associated with the Edinburgh clubs that met in taverns, they resolved to meet in the more wholesome atmosphere of their homes. Each would take turns acting as host, or "steward." Prominent members of the community were invited to attend meetings occasionally, and visitors to Annapolis from other states and countries were always welcome. Hamilton acted as secretary and kept detailed minutes of club meetings which afford us a wonderful insight into eighteenth-century humor, manners, and social conventions, as well as glimpses into the personalities of the club members.

Although the charter members were prominent merchants and lawyers, the Tuesday Club did not confine itself to the upper stratum of Annapolis society. Its membership included a number of tradesmen and mariners, as well as at least one tavern-owner, Samuel Middleton, whose establishment at the city dock catered to sailors and ship-builders.

Just six months after Green was initiated, he was made "deputy president" of the club, and he presided over the admission to membership of two fast-rising lawyers, Stephen Bordley and Thomas Jenings. Green proved himself useful in various ways. The club's forte was burlesque, both political and social. The president, Charles Cole, directed the proceedings from under a huge canopy in the shape of a scallop shell, upon which was fixed the shield and mottos of the club. The adoption of club bylaws was done with great formality, involving lengthy speeches and formal balloting. Green added to the mock solemnity by printing a set of ballots, "curiously done in the Shape of Little books." At Green's suggestion, the ballots were then cast by throwing them into a hat, so as to preserve each voter's secrecy. Discovering that Green had a talent for poetry, the club in March 1749 named him "Poet Laureat of the Tuesday Club" and charged him with drafting "a proper ode for the next Anniversary day of the Club, to be Sung by the Club's Musician." A month later his various offices and talents were officially recognized when the Club passed legislation styling Green "in the manner of Old Romans as follows, Jonas Green, Esq. P.P.P.P.P., Importing Sundry great offices of trust dignity and Importance, vizt. Poet, Painter, Punster, Purveyor, and Punchmaker General."

Although his verses lack appeal to the modern ear, Green was inordinately proud of his poetic talents. On one occasion he got himself into trouble by publishing a poem in his newspaper before presenting it to the president, Charles Cole (styled "His Lordship" in the minutes), in violation of the rules and laws of the club. He was subjected to a formal trial before the club membership and convicted. Secretary Hamilton recorded that, upon the sentence being given, "the Serjeant at arms Immediately Took Jonas Green, Esq. P. P. &c. into custody, and he was confined for a full half hour, a languishing prisoner in a remote corner of the Room, being deprived of all Comfort and assistance from the Sparkling and enlivening bowl, a woeful and lamentable Spectacle and example of his Lordship's Just displeasure, and a warning to all Loyal members to be upon their good behavior."

On the other hand, there was universal joy among club members when one of Green's poems, the ode for the year 1750, was published in the *Gentleman's Magazine* of London. Secretary Hamilton duly recorded the celebration:

> After Supper, the ode was performed with Several Instruments, and a voice, the march was accompanied with beat of Drum, while his Lordship and Sir John [styled in the minutes as "Champion & Knight of the Club"] Sat in State with their Swords drawn, and Sir John danced to his own minuet sword in hand.

The formation of a uniquely American character and personality was as important in the building of a nation as political independence. The Tuesday Club made its own contribution to this development by mocking both the pretentions of the Old World aristocracy and the American yearning for world acceptance. By blurring the lines of social class, it reflected the mobility of American society. Yet it also sought to educate the "mixed multitude" (Dr. Hamilton's phrase) in the ways of a cultured and enlightened society, a milieu in which art and music could be appreciated and ideas freely exchanged. Unfortunately, the club was too dependent upon the intellectual leadership of Dr. Hamilton, and it fell apart when he died in 1756.

Jonas Green and his *Gazette* contributed in quite another way to the democratization of Maryland politics. The average voter had previously been but little engaged in the political controversies of the 1730s and 1740s. Except for the brief tenure of Parks's *Gazette*, there had been no medium for political exchange outside the halls of the legislature. The public was aware of the din, through the proclamations of the governor and occasional pamphlets by the opposition, but it had no way of becoming engaged. Green began publishing the news of provincial affairs in his paper, just as Parks had done in the 1720s. In 1752, Green began printing on the front page of his paper the daily journal of the House of Delegates, exposing the voters to the political issues at stake and informing them of the positions taken by their representatives. After the French and Indian War broke out in 1756, Green further whetted the public interest in politics by publishing the legislative decision on war appropriations as well as the news of the military campaigns. By the end of the war, in the early 1760s, the lower house was routinely ordering that its annual appropriation bill be printed "for the perusal of the inhabitants." Individual members of the House pled their own cases under pseudonyms in the columns of the *Gazette*.

The Stamp Act of 1765 brought to an early head the growing connection between the press and popular politics. Journalists in every colony played a prominent role in opposition to the Stamp Act because newspapers were among the items to be taxed, but none of them was more expert in manipulating public opinion than Jonas Green. In the past he had only sparingly inserted his own opinions in the paper, but as the controversy over the Stamp Act exploded into violence he became increasingly bolder in his editorial comments. On April 18, 1765, while Parliament still had the act under consideration, Green informed his readers, between heavy, black mourning bars, that the newspaper, "Alas! must soon droop and expire, at least for some time, if the melancholy and alarming accounts, we have just heard from the northward, prove true, that an act of Parliament is shortly to take place, laying a heavy and insupportable *Stamp Duty* on all American gazettes &c, &c."

For the next six months every weekly edition of the *Gazette* carried news or discussion of the tax. Green copied liberally from the papers of northern cities, as well as the prints brought by packet vessel from London. On June 6 Green printed the famous address of opposition leader Isaac Barré, in which he informed the House of Commons that the colonists had originally fled to the New World to avoid English tyranny and that their descendants — "Sons of Liberty" — were seeking only to preserve their ancient freedom. Within days Green followed with the radical resolutions offered by Patrick Henry to the Virginia House of Burgesses, and in the middle of the summer he printed the invitation of the Massachusetts House of Representatives to attend the Stamp Act congress to be held in New York in October. Marylanders joined the newspaper controversy, using pseudonyms of militant defenders of the Roman republic. They discussed the constitutional limitations on the power of Parliament, as well as the injustice of the Stamp Act. On August 22 the *Gazette* announced that a stamp distributor had been appointed for Maryland, and it printed a letter from a "Gentleman in London" that described the glee with which parliament was cramping American trade and destroying the colonists' freedom. Referring to Isaac Barré's "sons of liberty" thesis, the "Gentleman" concluded: "Oh! degeneracy of ancient Britons! America! how thou art fallen!" Four days later the first public meeting, chaired by Samuel Chase, met in Annapolis to protest the Stamp Act. Several days of violence followed, in Annapolis, Baltimore, and about a dozen smaller communities in the colony.

Although the Maryland stamp distributor fled to New York — the first such departure in the southern colonies — Green kept up the pressure. On October 10, the date on which the ill-conceived legislation was to take effect, his journal bore the name *The Maryland Gazette, Expiring: In Uncertain Hopes of a Resurrection to Life again.* A week later he published the first of three "supplements" to that issue, thereby avoiding publishing a new edition that would be subject to the tax. On December 10 he maintained the fiction that his paper had been slain by British tyranny by publishing it under the name *An Apparition of the late Maryland Gazette.* The disappearance of the stamp collector, who ended up destitute in the West Indies, virtually nullified the act in Maryland, and on January 30, 1766, Green changed the name to *The Maryland Gazette, Reviving.* The paper resumed its old name and numbering on March 6. When news of the repeal of the act arrived on May 27, the *Gazette* reported that "Loyal and Patriotic Toasts were Drank, the Guns at the Dock at the same time Firing, and other Demonstrations of Joy shewn, on account of the IMPORTANT NEWS OF THE STAMP ACT being Repealed."

The Stamp Act was Jonas Green's last crusade. On April 16, 1767, the *Maryland Gazette* contained a notice that he had died (at the age of fifty-five) the previous Saturday at his dwelling house on Charles Street. The notice was accompanied by a plea from Anne Catherine Green for the continued patronage by the people of Maryland of her press and newspaper.

The printing trade was one of the few that was relatively open to women in the eighteenth century. Women operated presses and published newspapers in almost every colony, although most of them, like Anne Catherine Green, were widows carrying on the work of their husbands. Society nevertheless accepted this occupational outlet for women, probably because it was conducted indoors and in relative privacy. A single woman who conducted a trade on her own initiative was recognized in the law. They were known as "feme sole" traders. They could execute binding contracts, sue, and be sued — rights that married women did not have.

In his *Autobiography*, Benjamin Franklin noted that the most successful of his printing partnerships involved the widow of a journeyman whom Franklin had sent to Charleston, South Carolina. She sent regular accounts to Franklin and managed the business with such success that she purchased the Charleston printing shop from Franklin and established her son in it. Franklin thought the woman's success was due to her birth and education in Holland, where, Franklin was informed, "the knowledge of accounts makes a part of female education."

This background may also have been of advantage to Anne Catherine Green, for she picked up her husband's business without a public ripple. Assisted by her son William, who was probably in his late twenties, she completed the *Acts and Votes* of the assembly for the 1767 session. In its act for the encouragement of the public printer in 1768, the Assembly noted that she had performed satisfactorily the duties of printer to the province, and it paid her the sum of "Nine hundred and forty-eight dollars and one-half dollar." It further provided that for her future services as public printer she would receive 48,000 pounds of tobacco annually for those years in which there was an Assembly session and 36,109 pounds when the Assembly was not in session. The shift in payment from Maryland currency to gold (the dollar was a Spanish gold coin) and tobacco no doubt reflected the facts that Maryland had retired its wartime issues of paper, and that Parliament had prohibited the colonies from further issues of paper money.

The *Maryland Gazette* under Mrs. Green's management preserved its Whiggish political complexion. Between December 1767 and March 1768 she published in installments John Dickinson's *Letters from a Farmer in Pennsylvania*, which advanced the American constitutional argument a step farther by denying that Parliament had any revenue authority in America whatsoever. In the early 1770s the pages of her journal were filled every week with the controversy over the governor's fee proclamation.

The increasing bitterness with which political dialogue was conducted, however, forced her to adopt stronger policies with regard to publication. In 1766 her husband had rejected as "too personal" a letter by Samuel Chase attacking Annapolis Mayor Walter Dulany. The following year Mrs. Green refused to print arguments by the rector of Saint Anne's who wished to rid his vestry of elements opposed to him. The grounds for her refusal were that the rector refused to sign his essays or to post bond to indemnify the printer in the event of a libel suit. The policy on the part of Mrs. Green became even firmer after a run-in with William Paca in 1773. Upset over personal attacks on him in unsigned letters, Paca told Anne Catherine Green, in a letter she published, "if you are hereafter an instrument in propagating, thro' the channel of your press any *personal reflections* on me, and *conceal* the author, by which, as hithertoo, I am deprived of an opportunity of treating the *infamous scoundrel* in the manner he may deserve, I shall hold you responsible." Anne Catherine Green's policy thereafter was one followed by the American press to the present day: no personal or vindictive letters would be published, and no letter of any kind would be printed unless the real name of the author was conveyed to the printer.

William Green died in 1770. He could not have been much more than thirty years old, but we know nothing of his health history or illness. For the next two years Mrs. Green managed the shop by herself. As she gained experience the quality of her work improved and her reputation spread. The city commissioned her to print *The Charter and Bye-Laws of the City of Annapolis*, which one student of the printing art has described as "a beautifully printed little volume of fifty-two pages, which for typographical nicety could hardly have been surpassed by the best of her contemporaries in the colonies." From January 1772 until her death she functioned under the partnership name of Anne Catherine Green & Son, this son being Frederick. Nevertheless, in its annual appropriations, the Assembly designated Anne Catherine Green, and not the partnership, as the printer to the province.

By mid-1774, the columns of the *Gazette* were crowded with news of the crisis in Boston, stemming from the closure of the port after the Tea Party, and the popular meetings being held to protest the "intolerable acts." In the issue of June 2, Mrs. Green inserted an apologetic note: *"The conclusion of the essay on the advantages of a classicial education, is postponed for the want of room. — Advertisements omitted will be inserted next week."* During the autumn of 1774 the Greens turned their paper into an organ of the Anne Arundel committee of correspondence. They published notices of public meetings and advised of approaching elections. The proceedings of the provincial convention and the Continental Congress filled their pages. By choosing certain contributors over others, they turned the *Gazette* into an oracle of revolutionary fervor.

Unfortunately, Anne Catherine Green did not live to witness the Revolution. She died on March 23, 1775, a month before the battles at Lexington and Concord. The notice of her death in the *Maryland Gazette*, written no doubt by her son Frederick, concluded with the assurance that "she was of a mild and benevolent Disposition, and for conjugal affection and parental Tenderness, an Example to her Sex."

Frederick took over the paper and continued its militant support for the patriot cause. He suspended production from 1777 to 1779 due to a shortage of paper — the result, no doubt, of the British occupation of Philadelphia. The *Gazette* resumed publication on April 30, 1779, under the aegis of the partnership of Frederick & Samuel Green. The brothers continued to publish the paper until they died within a week of one another in 1811. Thereafter, Jonas Green, son of Samuel, carried the publication until its final issue in 1839. No other family dynasty in American history has carried on a single craft through so many generations. And few others have made such a signal contribution to the birth of the Republic.

Selected Reading

S tarting points for a study of Maryland society in the eighteenth century are two excellent books: Gloria L. Main, *Tobacco Colony: Life in Early Maryland, 1650–1720* (1982), and Allan Kulikoff, *Tobacco and Slaves: The Development of Southern Cultures in the Chesapeake, 1680–1800* (1986). Demanding, but nevertheless rewarding, are two collections of essays on the same subject. The first, edited by Aubrey C. Land, Lois Green Carr, and Edward C. Papenfuse, is entitled *Law, Society, and Politics in Early Maryland* (1974), and the second, a more recent collection edited by Lois Green Carr, Philip D. Morgan, and Jean B. Russo, is entitled *Colonial Chesapeake Society* (1988). A recent study of the adaptation of English people and culture to life in the Chesapeake is James Horn, *Adapting to a New World: English Society in the Seventeenth-Century Chesapeake* (1994). An ecological approach to the impact of colonization is Timothy Silver, *A New Face on the Countryside: Indians, Colonists, and Slaves in the South Atlantic Forests, 1500–1800* (1990).

The standard work on Maryland politics is Charles A. Barker, *Background of the Revolution in Maryland* (1940). This can be supplemented by two more recent works: Ronald Hoffman, *A Spirit of Dissension: Economics, Politics, and the Revolution in Maryland* (1973), and David C. Skaggs, *Roots of Maryland Democracy, 1753–1776* (1973). Edward C. Papenfuse, *In Pursuit of Profit: The*

Annapolis Merchants in the Era of the American Revolution, 1763–1805 (1975), focuses specifically on Annapolis in the Revolutionary era. For post-Revolutionary politics, see Norman K. Risjord, *Chesapeake Politics, 1780–1800* (1978).

Some of the individuals discussed in this book have been treated in full-length biographies. Among these are Aubrey C. Land, *The Dulanys of Maryland* (1955, repr. 1968); Joseph Gurn, *Charles Carroll of Carrollton, 1737–1832* (1932); Thomas O. Hanley, *Revolutionary Statesman: Charles Carroll and the War* (1983); James Haw, *Life of Samuel Chase* (1980), Gregory A. Stiverson and Phebe R. Jacobsen, *William Paca: A Biography* (1976); and William Voss Elder and Lu Bartlett, *John Shaw, Cabinetmaker of Annapolis* (1983).

Specialized studies have enlivened the stories of individual men. The story of Governor Nicholson's design for Annapolis benefits immensely from John W. Reps, *Tidewater Towns: City Planning in Colonial Virginia and Maryland* (1972) and from Edward C. Papenfuse, *"Doing Good to Posterity": The Move of the Capital of Maryland from St. Mary's City to Ann Arundel Towne, Now Called Annapolis* (1995), a pamphlet available at the Maryland Hall of Records in Annapolis. The description of Dr. Charles Carroll's medical practice draws heavily on Richard H. Shryock, *Medicine and Society in America, 1660–1860* (1960) and Douglas G. Carroll, Jr. *Medicine in Maryland, 1643–1900* (1984). For information on the Carroll House in Annapolis I am indebted to Ellen Craft, who gave a lecture on the subject in the spring of 1996. The insights into the unique nature of the Paca garden are those of Mark Leone, "William Paca's Power Garden: The Art of Illusion in Colonial Annapolis," in *Maryland Humanities* (July/August 1994), published by the Maryland Humanities Council in Baltimore. Lawrence C. Wroth, *History of Printing in Colonial Maryland* (1922) has a chapter on the Green family, and the anecdotal material in the essay on Jonas Green was derived from Elaine G. Breslaw, ed., *Records of the Tuesday Club of Annapolis, 1745–56* (1988). The Green chapter in this book is also indebted to David C. Skaggs, "Editorial Policies of the *Maryland Gazette*, 1765–1783," *Maryland Historical Magazine*, 59 (1964), 341–349.

Index

References to illustrations are printed in italic type.

INDEX

About the Author

Norman K. Risjord is professor of emeritus of American history at the University of Wisconsin–Madison. He is author of a series of books about "Representative Americans" and a biography of Thomas Jefferson. He divides his time between Annapolis and his farm in Wisconsin.

Designed by Gerard A. Valerio,
Bookmark Studio, Annapolis

Composed in Baker Signet and Sabon
by Sherri Ferritto, Typeline, Annapolis

Printed and bound by Thomson-Shore, Inc.,
Dexter, Michigan

Cover printed by Whitmore Print & Imaging,
Annapolis, Maryland